Glad

to

Forgive

Dr. Tom Mills

Unless otherwise noted, all Scripture references in this publication are from the New King James Version; Copyright ©1979, 1980, 1982, Thomas Nelson, Inc., publishers.

Printed in the United States of America.

ISBN: 0-9772850-2-2

Library of Congress Control Number: 2005910499

ORDERING INFORMATION:
Contact Tom Mills at tommills@ihop.org.

To:
Debbie, my wife,
and
our three wonderful children,
Marisa, Alicia, and Jonathan

Thank you all for
constantly demonstrating true
forgiveness to me. Without you I
would never have made it this far.

Acknowlegements

No book is ever conceived or produced in a vacuum. I must begin my offering of thanks with Dr. Bill Purdy. As a member of the congregation of Kingswood United Methodist Church in Amarillo, Texas, Bill encouraged me first to capture my teaching in a book. Bill, here it is — 15+ years later!

Then there is Dr. Anne Daghistany. Anne, my literature professor in the university over 30 years ago, inspired me more than she will ever know. When she re-entered my life as a member of St. Luke's United Methodist Church in Lubbock, Texas where I served as Senior Pastor, not only did she pick up where Dr. Purdy left off, she mentored me through much of the writing process.

In addition to those who inspire, there are also those who read rough and ugly first drafts. Thanks go to Elizabeth Matthews, Suzanne Wyss, and Sandy Hall for reading early manuscripts and making comments that helped shape the content and flow of the final work.

Finally, thank you Kris DeCanio for your work in doing the final editing and keeping me from making too many mistakes in public. Thanks also for pointing out a few "Texasisms" that some outside the Great State might not have understood. I have removed as many as I could without betraying my roots.

Contents

Introduction

Hinduism:

"Those men that ever conquer their wrath by forgiveness, obtain the higher regions. Therefore has it been said that forgiveness is the highest virtue."[1]

Islam:

"Thus must not forget that as much as we need Allah's forgiveness for our sins and mistakes, we must forgive those who do wrong to us."[2]

Buddhism:

"What is forgiving? It is refusing to let the past determine the present."[3]

Confucius:

"Those who cannot forgive others break the bridge over which they themselves must pass."[4]

Judaism:

"It is forbidden to be cruel and difficult to appease, rather, a person must be quick to forgive and difficult to anger and when the sinner asks for forgiveness he should forgive him willingly and wholeheartedly...."[5]

Wicca:

"Forgiveness is about letting go of ineffective and self-harming anger, healing your wounds, and creating a better you by learning the right lessons from your painful experience.."[6]

Forgiveness is something that almost everyone knows needs to happen. A look at those statements on the subject of forgiveness from some of the prevalent world religions and philosophies bears that out. Virtually every religion and philosophical system on the planet teaches some form of forgiveness -- even the witches of Wicca! And yet, we live in a culture that knows almost nothing of practicing forgiveness.

> Every religion and philosophical system on the planet teaches some form of forgiveness.

On May 7, 2004, Marilyn Logan's son, John Ekberg, was killed in a senseless act of road rage in the parking lot of a race track near Kansas City. When, at the end of the trial, the convicted assailant asked her forgiveness, she replied, "I have thought long and hard about whether I could forgive him. That is something he will have to seek from God. I can't grant it to him." You see, she knew she was supposed to forgive, she just wasn't able or willing to do it!

A recent Gallup poll indicated that 94% of Americans know the importance of forgiveness, and yet less than half actually do forgive! Arabs, Israelis, Blacks, Whites, Asians, Hispanics, Tribes, Nations, Cultures, Young, Old, Parents, Children, Brothers, Sisters, Husbands, Wives, Friends, Strangers, you name it and we are at each other's throats over conflicts and offenses that could be resolved if we would actually do what we know is right.

There are certainly many more statements about forgiveness that could be included here, but none is more significant or visual than the author of forgiveness, Jesus. As He hung on the cross, being tortured to death He said, *"Father, forgive them for they do not know what they do."* (Luke 23:34)

When I read these words of Jesus, when I think of the agony of the cross, when I consider that Jesus was completely innocent and never did anything to hurt or harm anyone, and yet, through bloody lips and labored breathing spoke forgiveness, I am taken to another passage of Scripture. *"Blessed are the merciful, for they shall obtain mercy."* (Matthew 5:7)

Blessed is more than general happiness. Our culture has so diluted the meaning of happiness that it no longer truly communicates what *blessed* means. *Blessed* is not just something that is felt on the inside. Instead, it is so pervasive that it is observable by others. The blessedness taught in the beatitudes is so much a part of the person's character and composition that it bubbles out onto everyone he or she contacts. It is not contrived. It is not manipulative. It is not something that the blessed person even thinks about. Blessedness describes an internal condition that shines beyond the one who possesses it. In fact, a person doesn't possess blessedness; blessedness possesses the person!

And when Jesus teaches that a merciful person is blessed, he is not telling us that a person is blessed because he is merciful. Not at all! He is telling us that a person is merciful because he is blessed! When a disciple of Jesus Christ realizes just what he has and who he is because of Jesus, the only possible response is a demonstration of mercy.

Now, what is mercy? Mercy is a heart attitude that inevitably is made manifest in actions. It is a sense of pity accompanied by a compelling desire to do something about it. In other words, a heart filled with mercy can't help itself -- it must extend mercy to anyone that offends, no matter how heinous the offense. In fact, mercy doesn't wait on an offense to occur; it extends mercy before it is offended. It might even be said that a merciful person actually hopes someone will offend just for the sheer joy or gladness that comes in extending mercy to the transgressor. There is such an internal blessedness—gladness— that comes from extending mercy, or forgiveness, that those in whom the Spirit of Jesus lives will show mercy with eagerness. "Blessed are the merciful" really says that a disciple of Jesus is glad to forgive! It is my prayer that this book will help us all become just that as we move through the process of becoming more like Jesus every day.

Chapter 1

The Danger: A Deadly Wound

Boys are bound to get hurt; it's almost a rite of passage. Cuts, scrapes and breaks are all part of growing up. At the age of 4, playing "Red Light - Green Light" in the back yard with the neighborhood kids, I skidded into the knee of a boy more than twice my age (imagine that, playing with someone as old as 10!) and came up with a real shiner. Three years later, I had another collision with the same kid (guess I'm a slow learner), this time on the baseball diamond. He was pitching, I was playing third base, and the pop up went between us. This was before the days of the infield fly rule, so someone had to catch it! When I awakened, I was on my back in the infield dirt, hearing one of the other kids say, "Hey, here's somebody's teeth!" I knew who that somebody was. Second grade and I learned that permanent teeth are not so permanent after all (and I never did find out if anyone actually caught the pop fly).

In that same year, I sustained another not-so-life-threatening injury. It may not have been serious, but it was painful, and it could have become serious, even life threatening if my parents had not insisted that a doctor take a look at my injury. Several of us guys had been playing around Thompson Ward Elementary School when I fell. I'm certain I was pushed, but no one would admit it. Even so, I fell and cut the palm of my hand. It bled like crazy! I knew that the only way for me to stop the bleeding was to head home and let my mom wash it, put some kind of burning orange stuff on it, and cover it with an adhesive bandage. I was certain my dad wouldn't be the one to dress the wound, he was not fond of blood and got queasy just thinking about it. Remember the black eye when I was four and the knocked out teeth when I was seven? My dad nearly passed out on both of those, so I was certain that mom would be the medic on call. Sure enough, that's exactly what happened. My mom cleaned and dressed the wound and sent me back outside to play.

That should have been the end of it. However, several weeks later the wound had mostly covered over with skin, but it was definitely not healed. It was hot, red, and throbbing with pain. Every time I touched it, lightning exploded through my hand and up to my elbow. My mom knew there must be something wrong, so she loaded me into our 1957 Chevrolet station wagon and we headed for Dr. Thompson's office. He was the local physician in our little North Central Texas community, and he took care of just about everyone. He took my throbbing hand in his and began to push all around the wound, as I squirmed with the pain.

Then he said, "I think there is something still in there. I'm going to have to open it."

I didn't like the sound of that. I didn't like it more when I saw the nurse bringing in a hypodermic needle. To my adolescent eyes, it was a big as those 16 penny nails we used to place on the railroad track just to watch the train smash them flat. But that's an entirely different story. I didn't like the looks of that needle, and it got worse when I saw a sharp scalpel resting beside the needle on a little tray.

He picked up the needle and my hand, and said, "This is going to sting a little." He flat out lied! It didn't sting a little; it hurt a lot! But then the shot took effect and my hand went numb. Next came the knife. I don't know what possessed me to watch. I can't figure out why my mom let me, but she did and I did. He made a very small incision right in the middle of the red wound. Then he reached for a steel rod and began to probe around in the now bleeding cut. I felt, or heard -- I can't remember which -- the probe scrape against something hard. I just knew the doc was digging all the way down to the bone. By now I was curious. No longer frightened or in pain, I watched with amazement as suddenly a little sliver of glass popped to the surface. He picked it up with some tweezers (he probably called them forceps) and put it on the tray, then probed a little longer just to be sure there were no more fragments in the cut.

Satisfied that it was clean, he disinfected it. I was pretty sure he was done and ready to put a bandage on it and send me home, when he brought out this little electric branding iron. "What are you going to do with that?" I panicked!

He assured me it would be ok, and I assure you that I stopped watching at that point. He applied the hot surface to my open wound and sealed it shut. I could smell burning flesh, but fortunately the anesthetic was still at work. The "branding" lasted only a couple of seconds, and then he put a bandage on the wound and sent me home.

> Fragments of unforgiveness lead to bitterness which poisons the entire system.

Today, I can look at my left palm and see the scar. There is no more pain. There is no diminishing of dexterity. But if my parents had not made me go to the doctor and let him dig out the thing that was creating the problem, there is a very real possibility that I could have lost my hand. Left untreated, blood poisoning could have set in, followed by gangrene, and eventually I could have lost my life. It seems ludicrous to think that anyone would let it go that far, to allow something alien to the human frame to remain embedded and create a dangerous even life threatening situation. And yet, people do it every day! Oh, these fragments that create the toxins that threaten life are not of a physical nature. They aren't wood or metal or glass. They are, however, even more deadly.

I'm talking about fragments of unforgiveness that lead to bitterness that poisons the entire system (body, soul, spirit) and ultimately can lead to sickness or even death. In the Gospel of John, Jesus encountered a man who had been paralyzed much of his life. I'm convinced that his paralysis resulted from fragments of unforgiveness that he allowed to poison his entire system. Let's look at the event as detailed in Chapter 5:1-15.

The legend of the day was that an angel would come down on an unscheduled, and unpredictable basis and stir up the wa-

John 5:1-15

1 After this there was a feast of the Jews, and Jesus went up to Jerusalem. 2Now there is in Jerusalem by the Sheep Gate a pool, which is called in Hebrew, Bethesda, having five porches. 3In these lay a great multitude of sick people, blind, lame, paralyzed, waiting for the moving of the water. 4For an angel went down at a certain time into the pool and stirred up the water; then whoever stepped in first, after the stirring of the water, was made well of whatever disease he had. 5Now a certain man was there who had an infirmity thirty-eight years. 6When Jesus saw him lying there, and knew that he already had been in that condition a long time, He said to him, "Do you want to be made well?"

7The sick man answered Him, "Sir, I have no man to put me into the pool when the water is stirred up; but while I am coming, another steps down before me."

(Continued on the next page)

8Jesus said to him, "Rise, take up your bed and walk." 9And immediately the man was made well, took up his bed, and walked. And that day was the Sabbath. 10The Jews therefore said to him who was cured, "It is the Sabbath; it is not lawful for you to carry your bed."

11He answered them, "He who made me well said to me, 'Take up your bed and walk.'

12Then they asked him, "Who is the Man who said to you, 'Take up your bed and walk'?" 13But the one who was healed did not know who it was, for Jesus had withdrawn, a multitude being in that place. 14Afterward Jesus found him in the temple, and said to him, "See, you have been made well. Sin no more, lest a worse thing come upon you."

15The man departed and told the Jews that it was Jesus who had made him well.

ters in this pool. Then whoever was the first to get into the water after it was stirred up would be healed. My guess is that the area around the pool looked something like the sun deck beside the swimming pool on a cruise ship only more clothes, less suntan oil, and not nearly as attractive. People would literally sleep there just in case the stirring came at night or early in the morning. One of those beside the pool was the man in question. I want to skip to the end of the story first, because Jesus tells the man something that doesn't seem to fit. He says, "See, you have been made well. Sin no more, lest a worse thing come upon you."

Doesn't that pique your curiosity? Don't you want to know what was his sin? Seriously, what was Jesus talking about here? When he healed the man, He didn't say, "Your sins are forgiven, rise and walk."

He didn't even mention sin in his first encounter with the man. So what exactly was Jesus talking about? I think we can figure it out with some simple observations.

First, this man had been 38 years in his sickness, 38 years paralyzed, 38 years enduring the scornful stares of people, 38 years with his ears filled with the sounds of children mocking, 38 years of adults ignoring him, 38 years (and I know this is very offensive, but you need to see the reality of this passage of Scripture) 38 years sitting in his own waste. Think about

> # Do you want to be made well?

it! If he couldn't find anyone to put him in the water, do you think he could find anyone to toilet him and to clean up after him? And John reports in Chapter 5 verse 6, that Jesus had the audacity to ask, "Do you want to be made well?"

It's a valid question, and one that people living with fragments of unforgiveness must answer. Do you want to be free of your disease, and if you don't want to be free, why not? Why would anyone possibly choose to sit for 38 years in their own waste when they could be up walking around living a more complete life? Could it be that they have grown so fond of self-pity that they don't quite know what they would do if it were gone?

A second observation is found in several verses; the first is verse 7. The sick man answered Him, *"Sir, I have no man to put me into the pool when the water is stirred up; but while I am coming, another steps down before me."* This man loved to shift the blame to others. He was not willing to assume the responsibility for his own actions. His response to Jesus' question tells it all. "It isn't my fault, I don't have anyone to help me, and only the speedy people get the healing."

This theory is further strengthened by verses 9-13. Here, the man got into trouble for carrying his mat on the Sabbath, and again he shifted the blame onto someone else. You see, it was considered work in Jesus' day to carry a mat used for sleeping.[7]   When confronted by the religious leaders, he immediately blamed his healer. The man didn't know who that healer was, but it is obvious that if Jesus had been around, this man would have had no hesitation in pointing him out. It was certainly not his fault that he was breaking the Sabbath law, it was the fault of the one that had healed him.

How many people are like that? How many people can never get along with a boss and it's always the fault of the boss? How many people never seem to have any lasting friendships but it's never their fault, it's the others? How many people abuse alcohol or drugs and blame life circumstances or other people? How many students fail and blame the professor instead of their poor study habits. The list could go on and on. And in every case, it's always someone else's fault.

Now we're back to verse 14. Jesus ran into the man again. The indication is that quite a bit of time had passed, perhaps a few weeks or possibly even a month or more. In that interaction, Jesus confronted the man, *"Stop sinning. You're well now, but if you don't change, you're going to be worse than before."*

The man's response is very revealing. The man didn't say, "Wow! Thanks for the insight. I know it will be tough, but I'll clean up my act right now." No, instead verse 15 indicates that he went straight to the authorities and ratted out Jesus.

After all these observations, what can we conclude? Apparently, this man had forgotten all about the healing, but he remembered getting into trouble. He was still mad at Jesus. He was still carrying a grudge. He was still bitter. The man had been healed of a 38-year paralysis, but his bitterness had kept him imprisoned. And that is the sin Jesus was talking about. This man had been paralyzed by bitterness. For 38 years he had allowed some kind of offense, a fragment of unforgiveness, to live inside him, festering, poisoning his entire system. Jesus had given him a second chance, an opportunity to allow the great physician to probe deep into his wounded spirit and extract whatever was creating the toxin that had paralyzed him in the first place, and he was in the process of blowing it again. Jesus wanted him to be set free, but he refused.

Does this sort of thing happen in today's world? Let me tell you the story of two sisters. Janet was the older of the two, Sharon was the younger. Janet and Sharon grew up in a home of very devoted Christians, so much so that their dad was a top leader in their congregation for many years, and their mom was involved in every aspect of church life. They even had an uncle that was a member of the clergy in their denomination. They were raised in church with a strong belief in God.

Time passed. Janet and Sharon grew into young women. Both attended university. Janet received a degree in physical therapy. Sharon became a nurse practitioner. Both had a longing to help people who were hurting and in need of strength. Both married. Janet married a strong football player. Sharon a brilliant accountant. Janet had three children, all girls. Sharon had three children, two daughters and a son. After marrying, Janet moved to Phoenix; Sharon to New York City.

For years, their lives seemed to go on in a relatively normal fashion, though there were signs that all was not right. Janet seemed to have a lot of nervous problems. She smoked heavily and became quite dependent on alcohol. Her children seemed to have difficulty finding their way. Her oldest daughter was constantly worried and found her worth only in perfect performance. Her middle daughter became an alcoholic. She wandered around in complete insecurity and fear. She could never measure up to the perfect performance of her older sister so she never tried. Janet's third child, a girl, was a constant discipline problem and caused her much pain. Sharon's life seemed to be less chaotic than Janet's, and her children showed few signs of insecurity and fear beyond normal childhood fears.

In the course of time, Janet's hearing began to diminish. She would sit in silence, drink in hand, cigarette between her fingers, and just disconnecting from life. Her family tried to get her to seek some kind of professional help which she did.

Sharon also had some nagging uncertainties in her life. She was unsettled a lot of the time. She felt that something was wrong or missing, a sense of being incomplete, but she couldn't quite figure it out. So she, like her sister, sought outside guidance.

Ironically, almost eerily, it was in those sessions that they both discovered a memory that had been locked inside for years. Their uncle, the pastor, had molested them as little girls. He began with Janet, and after each time, he told her that she couldn't tell anyone or God would punish her. And what's more, if she told, he would just deny it, after all, "Who will people believe, a little girl with a vivid imagination, or a devout, respected member of the clergy?"

Janet remained silent and the memory was buried under a deep pile of denial for years. It was so deeply buried that she lost any conscious recollection, but her rage burned inside. When Sharon came along, she began to receive the same treatment from her uncle with the same instructions. She, too, buried her pain under fear and shame.

When the counseling revealed the hidden memories of abuse and intimidation, Janet had the opportunity to forgive, but she chose not to. Instead of letting it go, she turned it toward others, even her parents, accusing them of making the abuse possible, of protecting her uncle. They knew nothing of the abuse, yet she insisted they did. For a while, the family seemed to come apart. You can imagine that family life for everyone involved was hell over the next few years. The family became fragmented, filled with accusations, shame, and blame.

Sharon had a different reaction to the revelation of abuse than Janet. She worked through her pain, forgave her uncle, and has blossomed into a kind, loving, compassionate wife and mother committed to bringing healing and wholeness to people everywhere. She has a relationship with Christ and serves him through her church in New York. At one time she even toyed with the idea of becoming a pastor herself, but she realized that she was not called to that -- she would only be doing it to gain some kind of revenge against her uncle. When she recognized her wrong motives and some fragments of unforgiveness still in her system, she immediately let it go and now lives in more freedom every day. It was evident that she had truly forgiven when her abusive uncle attended the funeral for the father of Janet and Sharon. Sharon was able to be cordial to him and continue to function as a healer for those in attendance that were grieving the loss of their father and friend.

At her dad's funeral, Janet, on the other hand, was unable to be in the same room with the uncle. She was a total wreck because of grief over the death of her father, and yet she still held him responsible for not protecting her from the abusive uncle. She never quite recovered from that.

As she reached her middle fifties, Janet began to notice pain in her abdominal area, but she didn't go to the doctor to get it checked out. Then, in her 55th year, she had a heart attack. They rushed her to the hospital and discovered that she had two blocked arteries. While she was in coronary care, the tests they were running indicated that something else was going on in her body. CT scans revealed a mass in her abdomen that turned out to be a malignant tumor. They performed bypass surgery and planned to get to the treatment of her cancer after she was recovered enough to endure it.

Those treatments never came. Janet gained only enough strength to be moved from the Coronary Care Unit into hospice care. There she stayed for several weeks, gradually losing strength. In those last weeks, her family gathered around her, comforting her, encouraging her, praying for her. The day came when Janet entered into a "stupor-like" condition, caused by pain medication, and there she lingered. Days turned into weeks, no food or water was given her, and finally, she entered into eternity long before the 70 or 80 years promised us in Scripture.

When we contrast Janet's life, or lack of life, with that of her younger sister, Sharon, we begin to see the devastating effects of unforgiveness and the freeing effects of letting go. I have no objective evidence, but I am convinced that Janet died sooner than she should have because she refused to forgive. Sharon, on the other hand, is becoming wiser spiritually because she has chosen to forgive.

Each of us, as we travel through life, picks up many splinters. Some of them are our own fault. Some of them come because someone pushed us down, perhaps in a very violent way. And if the wounds are left unattended, they will not just go away. They will fester, create great pain, and can even cause physical sickness and death. But there is a solution. It is preferable to deal with splinters as they occur, but there are ways to get out even the most devastating of hurts that have been covered over for years. The remainder of this book will help us cleanse the wounds and move toward healing.

Chapter 2

The Problem: Sin

Ralph Waldo Emerson once said, "Can anybody remember when the times were not hard and money not scarce?" Mark Twain put it this way, "December is the toughest month of the year. Others are July, January, September, April, November, May, March, June, October, August, and February." Scott Peck, on the first page of his book, *The Road Less Traveled*, says, "Life is a series of problems." In other words, hardships, difficulties, and irritations are as much a part of life as breathing. But the fact that we humans continue to think that life is somehow supposed to be fair and easy points to the truth that difficulties and irritations are not part of the original design. God did not create us for hardship and conflict; He created us to behold beauty and enjoy His presence and the company of each other. He created us to live in joy and peace and harmony and love! So where did this offense thing get started? How did we human beings come to be offended by the silliest things, things like the particular sound of a person's voice, or the way someone laughs, or a person's ability to say and do particularly unintelligent things? Where did the bent to irritability come from?

Let's take a little trip back to The Garden -- Eden, that is. Throughout Scripture, and especially in the creation narratives, God revealed Himself mostly in terms of the relationship between Himself and humans. God created humankind to be in relationship with Him. He described that relationship in terms of marriage, something only humans could understand. God wanted a bride for His Son. He wanted someone with whom He could share the expanse of eternity in the context of time and space and joy and

> # Humankind was intended to live in complete friendship with God, self, and others

creativity. He wanted someone to respond to His affections with mutual affection. In order for God to express Himself fully, He created an object of affection, humankind.

Genesis 2 emphasizes the affectionate relationship between God and humans. Think of the language God used in portraying the original creation. God gave us trees that are *"pleasant to the sight and good for food."* (2:9); *"every green herb for food"* (1:30); *"a river went out of Eden to water the garden"* (2:10); and in the very center of it all there was *"the tree of life"* (2:9). This is the place mankind was intended to live in complete friendship with God, with himself, with others, and with creation. There was utter absence of conflict. God loved humankind. God loved all of creation and said that it was good. Humans loved God and enjoyed being in His company. Adam and Eve were in complete union with each other, neither was ever irritated with the other. Humans got along well with each other and with the whole of created order. There were no weeds to battle, no hail storms to dread, no earthquakes to fear. God and His creation were flowing together in a dance of perfection, turning and swirling in perfect unison, never stepping on each other's toes. It was marvelous. It was fun. It was exhilarating.

But obviously something went terribly wrong. A man and woman, who never felt disgrace, were suddenly ashamed and had to cover themselves. *"Then the eyes of both of them were opened, and they knew that they were naked; and they sewed fig leaves together and made themselves coverings"* (Genesis 3:7). The accord our original parents shared with self and others was shattered. Internal conflict prevailed. The man and woman, who were content to live in the bliss of Eden, suddenly found themselves wandering hopelessly outside the presence of God. Psalm 38:8 describes man now: *"I am feeble and severely broken; I groan because of the turmoil in my heart."*

A man and woman, who were totally open with God, suddenly felt the need to hide from Him. *"And they heard the sound of the LORD God walking in the garden in the cool of the day, and Adam and his wife hid themselves from the presence of the LORD God among the trees of the garden"* (Genesis 3:8). Friendship with God came to an end.

Plants that once were supportive of human life and were good for food became adversarial thorns and thistles. Animals that were would-be companions became predators. The earth that once freely shared its bounty with the humans became hostile and withheld its goodness.

> *Cursed is the ground for your sake;*
> *In toil you shall eat of it*
> *All the days of your life.*
> *Both thorns and thistles it shall bring forth for you,*
> *And you shall eat the herb of the field.*
> *In the sweat of your face you shall eat bread*
> *Till you return to the ground,*
> *For out of it you were taken;*
> *For dust you are,*
> *And to dust you shall return."*
>
> Genesis 3:17-19

Agreement with the natural world was broken.

But that was not God's intent; God never intended for us to have difficulty relating to Him. He never intended for earthquakes, tornados, hurricanes, droughts, and floods to devastate us. He never intended that we have neuroses and psychoses, and He never wanted us to hate each other. But those things do exist; the friendship and affection for which we were created has been broken. The flawless fabric of the universe has been soiled and torn.

Conflict with God, self, others and nature is the reason life is difficult, and the source of that conflict is found in the end of Genesis chapter 3. Verse 23 reveals an act that is totally opposed to the intentions God had for mankind. *"Therefore the LORD God sent him out of the garden of Eden to till the ground from which he was taken."* It was never intended that God should have to guard the tree of life from these rebellious creatures. He never desired to banish them from Eden. They were created for full partnership and friendship with God, self, each other, and nature. But in a matter of moments, all of that changed, and the kindest thing God could have done was to prevent them from touching the tree of life (Genesis 3:24). Can you imagine how terrible it would have been if humankind had been sentenced to eternity in its now broken state with no hope of redemption and reconciliation? Can you imagine having to live forever in terror of God rather than intimate affection and joy? Can you imagine eternity in shame and in personal conflict? Can you imagine time without end in the curse of constantly having to strive against natural disasters? Oh, what a blessing it was for our merciful God to limit our exposure to all this brokenness. So how did the agreement become disagreement? How was the harmony changed to disharmony? How did irritation and offense enter the blissful existence of Eden? The answer is a real life drama.

The Players

There are three main players in this drama: God, humans, and the serpent. We've already been introduced to God and the humans. The serpent is the new guy.

Revelation 12:9
So the great dragon was cast out, that serpent of old, called the Devil and Satan, who deceives the whole world; he was cast to the earth, and his angels were cast out with him.

In Revelation 12:9 and John 8:44 he is identified as the Devil or Satan. Isaiah 14:12-17 (on the next page) shows us that the serpent was a little too big for his britches and wanted to overthrow the Almighty Himself. Talk about an ego! But that attempted coup d'état was a trifle too ambitious. Such audacity!

John 8:44
You are of your father the devil, and the desires of your father you want to do. He was a murderer from the beginning, and does not stand in the truth, because there is no truth in him. When he speaks a lie, he speaks from his own resources, for he is a liar and the father of it.

When it didn't happen, the Devil changed tactics. Since he couldn't touch God directly, he determined to do the only thing he could to hurt God, to inflict as much pain and sorrow as possible. He determined to rob God of the affection humans had for Him. If the Devil could get the humans to believe that God was not all that special, and turn their love for God into self love and perhaps even love for him, then he could put a spike right through God's heart. If Satan could keep the humans from a lasting, loving, fulfilling relationship with God, if Satan could get Adam and Eve to think somehow that God even despised them, then he would be successful in hurting God.

Isaiah 14:12-17

12 "How you are fallen from heaven, O Lucifer, son of the morning! How you are cut down to the ground, You who weakened the nations! 13For you have said in your heart: 'I will ascend into heaven, I will exalt my throne above the stars of God; I will also sit on the mount of the congregation On the farthest sides of the north; 14I will ascend above the heights of the clouds, I will be like the Most High."15 Yet you shall be brought down to Sheol, To the lowest depths of the Pit. 16Those who see you will gaze at you, And consider you, saying: 'Is this the man who made the earth tremble, Who shook kingdoms, 17Who made the world as a wilderness And destroyed its cities, Who did not open the house of his prisoners?'

Satan hasn't changed tactics in all these millennia since. He doesn't care about you or me, personally. We are only tools he wants to use to hurt God. He is only using us to get to God. Where do you think criminals got the idea of kidnapping a child to get to the wealthy parents? Or what do you think inspired terrorists to abduct or kill ordinary citizens in order to hurt the government of the country they hate? The serpent had the idea first. Satan seeks to get to God by turning His children, His pride and joy, the objects of His deepest affection, away from Him. And how does he do that? He is successful by causing us to dwell in conflict with each other rather than unity.

In John 17:20-24 we find that God receives glory when we live in harmony or agreement with him and with each other. The world looks at our love for God and for each other and they marvel. In their wonder and desire for the same kind of harmony in their lives, they too come into relationship with God. God is overjoyed at that, and His glory shines throughout the land! The enemy will do everything he can to create conflict among God's people, destroy our unity, and keep God from receiving the glory He deserves and desires.

John 17:20-24

20 "I do not pray for these alone, but also for those who will believe in Me through their word; 21that they all may be one, as You, Father, are in Me, and I in You; that they also may be one in Us, that the world may believe that You sent Me. 22And the glory which You gave Me I have given them, that they may be one just as We are one: 23I in them, and You in Me; that they may be made perfect in one, and that the world may know that You have sent Me, and have loved them as You have loved Me. 24'Father, I desire that they also whom You gave Me may be with Me where I am, that they may behold My glory which You have given Me; for You loved Me before the foundation of the world.'

The good news is we can begin to spoil his efforts by knowing the tricks he will use to get us into conflict with each other and with him. Ephesians 6:11 warns us about the *"wiles of the Devil."* 1 Peter 5:8 describes that activity of Satan as *a roaring lion roaming about seeking someone to devour.* Then in verse 9 Peter gives a strong warning, *"Resist him, steadfast in the faith ..."*

Now, we come to an important question, HOW? How is it done? I mean, after all, if Adam and Eve, who knew God far more intimately than we do, could be tricked, then how can we ever hope to be smart enough to stand firm in our faith? The answer becomes clearer when we examine the nature of temptation. In Luke 22:40 Jesus makes an interesting comment. He is about to enter into the most devastating period of His short life. He is just hours away from betrayal, mock trial, humiliation and agonizing death by crucifixion. He and His companions have enjoyed one last meal together, and as was His custom, Jesus headed for the Garden of Gethsemane for prayer after supper. He would enter into great travail in just a few moments. But at the beginning of His trauma, He cautioned the disciples to pray that they *"not enter into temptation."* Then in verse 46 He pointed again to the need to *"pray, lest you enter into temptation."*

That seems like a strange prayer for this situation. What would be the nature of that temptation? Would it be the temptation to commit some horrible crime, some immoral act, some action we normally associate with sin? Probably not! Jesus wasn't concerned that these disciples would go off and commit some sinful action. He wasn't talking about stealing, or killing, or lying, or sexual lusting, or any of the actions we often associate with temptation. He was talking about something much deeper. He was talking about the root cause of all those sinful actions. He was talking about something that would cause them to not be able to be *"steadfast in the faith."* (1 Peter 5:8)

Jesus had spent the last three years of His life and ministry teaching these men about the God who was faithful, loving, and generous. The temptation they were about to face would be designed to lead them into a misunderstanding of the extravagant and passionate love of God, the Father. In truth, temptation is anything that distracts you from being in a relationship of extravagant love with God, anything that attempts to draw you away from believing or trusting in God's passionate love for you.

It was God's desire from the beginning that man share pleasure and delight with Him. But when life's events take a turn for the worse it's hard for us to see that delight. And when circumstances make it hard for us to see that we are the objects of God's delight, we become vulnerable to the temptation to be dragged away from God or distracted from our relationship with Him. So, this prayer might better be stated something like this: Pray that the enemy will not be able to use the events you are about to go through to change your understanding of God's loving nature and hurt your relationship with Him. Or to use Peter's words, pray that you will be able to be *"steadfast in the faith." Faith* here is the right belief about God.

In the coming hours, these followers of Jesus would face the most traumatic and frightening events they could ever imagine. The one temptation they were about to face would be the overwhelming urge to reject the God of extravagant love, to re-evaluate what they believed about God, to reject true *faith*. Satan would tempt them to change their beliefs about God. He would try to create conflict between them and God. And in so doing, he would succeed in hurting God.

THE CONTENT OF THE TEMPTING

A cursory examination of the interaction between the serpent and Eve reveals that he tried to change three of Adam and Eve's beliefs about God. He first attacked God's love and goodness. When the serpent said, "God knows that in the day you eat of it your eyes will be opened, and you will be like God," he was implying that God doesn't really love you because

He is holding you back from attaining your full potential. He could not be good nor loving if He would do something like that.

After getting Eve to question God's character, His goodness and love, the serpent then attacked God's faithfulness. When Eve told the serpent that they would die if they ate the fruit of the tree of knowledge of good and evil, the serpent immediately reacted, *"Surely you will not die!"* The implication of that statement was, "God is a liar! If He told you that you would die when He knows you won't die at all, but will in fact become better, He can't be trusted!"

Finally, the serpent even implied that God was not really God. You see, if man has the potential to be like God, then God can't be one of a kind, He can't be unique; and if He is not unique, He is not really

Genesis 3:1-6

1 Now the serpent was more cunning than any beast of the field which the LORD God had made. And he said to the woman, "Has God indeed said, 'You shall not eat of every tree of the garden?' 2 And the woman said to the serpent, "We may eat the fruit of the trees of the garden; 3 but of the fruit of the tree which is in the midst of the garden, God has said, 'You shall not eat it, nor shall you touch it, lest you die.'" 4 Then the serpent said to the woman, "You will not surely die. 5 For God knows that in the day you eat of it your eyes will be opened, and you will be like God, knowing good and evil." 6 So when the woman saw that the tree was good for food, that it was pleasant to the eyes, and a tree desirable to make one wise, she took of its fruit and ate. She also gave to her husband with her, and he ate.

God! If God is not really God at all, then the serpent attacked God's ability to do what He had promised.

The serpent created conflict between humans and God by getting Eve to believe three lies: God is not good or loving; God is not faithful, He can't be trusted; and God is not really God and therefore He doesn't have the ability to do what He said He would do. Eve was not "steadfast in the faith," to use Peter's words. It's interesting that Satan tried to get Jesus to believe the same three lies during His time of tempting in the wilderness.

THE TEMPTATION OF JESUS

Immediately following His baptism, Jesus was led into the wilderness by the Holy Spirit to be tempted by the Devil. The First Temptation, where the Devil attacks God's goodness, His love, is found in Matthew 4:1-3.

Matthew 4:1-3
1 Then Jesus was led up by the Spirit into the wilderness to be tempted by the Devil. 2And when He had fasted forty days and forty nights, afterward He was hungry. 3Now when the tempter came to Him, he said, "If You are the Son of God, command that these stones become bread."

That accusation could be seen as the classic question that comes to us in times of trouble, pain, or need, "If God loves you, why ...?" At His baptism, Jesus had heard His Father say, *"You are My beloved Son."* Now, after 40 days of fasting, Satan came to Jesus and said, "If God really loves You, why does He let you remain so hungry? Maybe God doesn't love You at all or things wouldn't be so bad. You must fend for yourself, so turn these stones into bread." You see, the first place Satan tempts us, the first place he desires to distract us from the faith, the first attempt to draw us away from what we know to be true of God, is in the area of His love. "If God really loved you, you wouldn't have the great unfulfilled need. If God really loved you, He wouldn't allow you to go on hurting as you are."

> If you don't know how precious you are to God, then you are vulnerable to being drawn away by the enemy.

Several years ago a friend of mine was in an oil field accident. My friend wasn't wearing a hard hat, when suddenly a heavy piece of equipment fell from a hundred feet above him, crashed right onto his head, fracturing his skull. They rushed him to the hospital, and as he lay in the bed in intensive care, through foggy eyes he looked up at me and asked, "If God is supposed to love me, why did this happen?" My friend survived the accident with no major ill effects, but in the traumatic event, the prowling lion sought to devour him by calling God's love into question. And if he can get us to truly believe that God doesn't love us, he can get us to break our relationship with Him and in so doing, hurt God.

The second temptation, the place where Satan tries to get us to re-evaluate our beliefs about God is related to His faithfulness.

Matthew 4:5

5 Then the Devil took Him up into the holy city, set Him on the pinnacle of the temple, 6and said to Him, "If You are the Son of God, throw Yourself down.

Satan took Jesus up to the pinnacle, the highest point, of the temple, and in effect, said, "If You are the Son of God, if God is really faithful to You, then jump from here because He said He would take care of You no matter what." Satan is challenging Jesus to prove God's faithfulness, and he does that by trying to put us into situations in which God appears to fail or disappoint us.

My wife, Debbie, and I have to fight this temptation in the area of giving. The Bible promises that if we will bring the whole tithe into the storehouse, God will pour out so much blessing on us that we will not be able to contain it all. *"Try Me now in this," says the Lord."* (Malachi 3:10) So we tithe and tithe and tithe, year after year we tithe, and still our bills seem to hang over us like threatening clouds. And a cascade of unexpected bills come -- medical bills, car repairs, plumbing problems, nothing frivolous or luxurious, just every day things that are not fun at all! And we are tempted to think that God has failed to keep his promises, that He isn't faithful!

This is a most powerful temptation, and one in which Jesus Himself nearly got trapped. As Jesus hung on the cross, He cried out, *"My God, My God, why have you forsaken me?"* (Matthew 27:46; Mark 15:34). The night before He was crucified, Jesus had prayed, *"Oh My Father, if it is possible, let this cup pass from me."* (Matthew 26:39; Mark 14:36; Luke 22:42). And now, it was obvious that God had not answered that prayer in the way Jesus hoped. The essence of his cry from the cross is, "Why have you left my cry for help unanswered? Why have you not been faithful to me? Why have you failed me?" He didn't stay long in that attitude, but since Jesus was fully human, He had *"... made himself of no reputation, taking the form of a servant, and coming in the likeness of men;"* (Philippians 2:7), He was tempted by this attack of the evil one.

If Satan fails in his attempt to distract us from God's love, and if he can't draw us away from God's faithfulness, then he has one more weapon in his arsenal. He will attack God's ability. He will try to convince us that God isn't really God at all,

Matthew 4:8-9

8 Again, the Devil took Him up on an exceedingly high mountain, and showed Him all the kingdoms of the world and their glory. 9 And he said to Him, "All these things I will give You if You will fall down and worship me."

and therefore, He has no ability to help us when life falls apart.

Satan said to Jesus, "I'll give you all the kingdoms of the world, if you'll just worship me." In other words, "Jesus, don't you know God isn't really God? Don't you know He can't deliver? You will never have what God promised you, because God is weak and doesn't even have the ability to do what He promised. Why don't you give up on God, and worship me?"

People that are sick for extended amounts of time are especially vulnerable here. People that have loved ones who are sick have trouble here. Broken relationships, hard marriages, or marriages where one spouse is not a believer are in places of particular vulnerability. If you don't know how precious you are to God, and if God hasn't answered your prayers in the particular way you wanted, then you are especially vulnerable to the drawing away of the enemy of God. Can't you just hear him? Hasn't the enemy ever told you that things were hopeless? Hasn't he ever gotten you to the point of discouragement so that you wanted to quit? Even for a fleeting moment? Have you ever doubted God's ability?

Satan tempts us to reject our heavenly Father at the point of His love, His faithfulness, and His divinity. If Satan can get us to believe that God doesn't love and care about the injustices that come our way, if he can cause us to believe that God can't be trusted to bring justice into unjust situations, and if he can get us to believe that God doesn't even have the ability to bring justice into a situation or conflict, then he can trick us into taking matters into our own hands. He can make us think we have to take care of ourselves. He can fool us into trying to become our own gods and to hand out our own form of justice.

It is at that point that we die and conflict begins to rule in our lives. When we look at the death that occurred in the garden, we find the root of every conflict

> Adam and Eve were convinced that God was not good, that God was not faithful, and that God was not really even God.

we now experience. Tragically, Adam and Eve didn't just experience one death, they suffered six deaths.

In Genesis 3:7, they realized they were naked. This was death of innocence. No longer could they look at each other with purity and peace. Now it is important to understand here that I am not talking about some kind of Puritanical understanding of sexuality, nor am I implying some kind of philosophical bent that the body is evil. The shame came when they realized they had lost the glory of God.

When we view the whole of Scripture, we realize that whenever a person spent any time in the presence of God, they came away with a holy glow. When Moses came down from the mountaintop, after having been in the presence of God for 40 days, his face was radiant.

Exodus 34:29-35
29 Now it was so, when Moses came down from Mount Sinai (and the two tablets of the Testimony were in Moses' hand when he came down from the mountain), that Moses did not know that the skin of his face shone while he talked with Him. 30So when Aaron and all the children of Israel saw Moses, behold, the skin of his face shone, and they were afraid to come near him. 31Then Moses called to them, and Aaron and all the rulers of the congregation returned to him; and Moses talked with them. 32Afterward all the children of Israel came near, and he gave them as commandments all that the LORD had spoken with him on Mount Sinai. 33And when Moses had finished speaking with them, he put a veil on his face. 34But whenever Moses went in before the LORD to speak with Him, he would take the veil off until he came out; and he would come out and speak to the children of Israel whatever he had been commanded. 35And whenever the children of Israel saw the face of Moses, that the skin of Moses' face shone, then Moses would put the veil on his face again, until he went in to speak with Him.

Angels glow because they have been in the presence of God. This is especially obvious in the announcement of the birth of Jesus to the shepherds, recorded in Luke 2:9, *"And behold, an angel of the Lord stood before them, and the glory of the Lord shone around them ...."* When Jesus met Moses and Elijah on the Mount of Transfiguration, they glowed. Jesus' *"clothes became shining,"* Mark 9:3 says. And Matthew 17:5 records the same event like this, *"While he was still speaking, behold, a bright cloud overshadowed them; and suddenly a voice came out of the cloud,* saying, *"This is My beloved Son, in whom I am well pleased. Hear Him!"*

Now if that is reality, and I am certain it is, then we can also understand that Adam and Eve lived in the presence of a holy glow. Because they spent time every day in direct contact with God, they were bound to have been glowing with His glory; and not only them, but the entire Garden must have been dazzling with the glory of God. But the moment they re-evaluated their belief about God, the moment they decided that God didn't love them, that God wasn't faithful, and that God wasn't really as good at being God as they could be, the moment they stepped into rebellion, that glow departed. Adam had never seen Eve without a holy glow. Eve had never seen Adam without glowing holiness. It was such a shock to their system that they tried to regain the glow. They tried to get the glow back. They noticed that the plants were still glowing (in similar fashion to the burning bush out of which God spoke to Moses in Exodus 3:2), so they sewed leaves together and hung them all over their bodies, not to cover their ugly bodies, but in order to get the glow back!

However, no artificial means could substitute for the real thing. The glory of God had departed and they were consumed with shame. They had squandered the gift God had given them and they died to purity and innocence and were consumed with internal conflict.

The second way they died is found in Genesis 3:8.

And they heard the sound of the LORD God walking in the garden in the cool of the day, and Adam and his wife hid themselves from the presence of the LORD God among the trees of the garden.

When the man and woman hid from God they revealed a broken relationship with God, their friendship was more than strained, it was broken. They experienced the death of security and peace. Paul describes it like this, *"For to be carnally minded is death, but to be spiritually minded is life and peace. Because the carnal mind is enmity against God ... So then, those who are in the flesh cannot please God."* (Romans 8:6-8)

In their inner being, Adam and Eve no longer felt it was possible to please God. They felt that God hated them. They no longer felt His pleasure. And even though God still desperately loved them, and longed for a relationship with them, they could not feel His delight. They began to live in fear. Security and peace had died.

A third way that Adam and Eve died is seen in Genesis 3:16. *"Your desire shall be for your husband, and he shall rule over you."* That spells the death of oneness and equality. The original pronouncement, *"They shall become one flesh"* (Genesis 2:24), had nothing of inequality in it. There is no sense of one being less or better than the other. Man and woman were one with absolutely no conflict, only total agreement. Then they changed their view of God. The enemy convinced them that God was not good, that God was not faithful, and that God was not really even God. Based on those lies, the first couple rebelled, and ushered in the death of equality and oneness inaugurating disagreement or conflict with others.

As if that were not enough, the fall into death continued in 3:17-19.

17 Then to Adam He said, "Because you have heeded the voice of your wife, and have eaten from the tree of which I commanded you, saying, 'You shall not eat of it'

> *Cursed is the ground for your sake;*
> *In toil you shall eat of it*
> *All the days of your life.*
> *18 Both thorns and thistles it shall bring forth for you,*
> *And you shall eat the herb of the field.*
> *19 In the sweat of your face you shall eat bread*
> *Till you return to the ground,*
> *For out of it you were taken;*

For dust you are,
And to dust you shall return."

The earth became an adversary rather than an ally. Adam and Eve experienced the death of material happiness as conflict with nature began. The glow of God's presence that had been on the trees and bushes of the garden was now removed. Where there had been no weeds, suddenly there were *"both thorns and thistles."* They died to the pleasure for which God had created them. The garden was supposed to be a place where they could enjoy God, for that is why they were created. But now, there would be floods and drought, earthquakes and tornados, freezing cold and scorching heat. Pleasure in the presence of God had died.

Loss of access to the tree of life signaled the next type of death experienced by Adam and Eve -- spiritual death.

22 Then the LORD God said, "Behold, the man has become like one of Us, to know good and evil. And now, lest he put out his hand and take also of the tree of life, and eat, and live forever" 23 therefore the LORD God sent him out of the garden of Eden to till the ground from which he was taken.

The conflict with God was now sealed and complete. No longer could the couple expect to meet with God in the cool of the day. No longer did they walk with Him. No longer were they able to talk easily to Him. They would be connected only by rituals and rules. According to Paul in Romans 1:20-21, their hearts became hard and unresponsive. Their

Romans 1:20-21

20 For since the creation of the world His invisible attributes are clearly seen, being understood by the things that are made, even His eternal power and Godhead, so that they are without excuse, 21 because, although they knew God, they did not glorify Him as God, nor were thankful, but became futile in their thoughts, and their foolish hearts were darkened.

spirits began to wither and die until the days of walking in the garden in the cool of the evening, enjoying intimacy with God, were nothing more than a fleeting memory, at best. The next stage of death actually was a blessing far preferable than living eternally in this fractured condition.

Finally, physical death arrived. Within one generation of the Devil convincing Adam and Eve that God was not good, that God was not faithful, and that God was not really even God, their firstborn, Cain, killed his little brother, Abel. Physical death is the final proof that the enemy's goal was to create conflict. And that conflict would keep God's pride and joy from coming together in unity. And without unity, God cannot receive the glory He deserves.

Chapter 3

The Solution: The Cross

In the last chapter, we learned where conflict originated. Over the aeons since our original parents introduced sin and conflict to the earth, we have become accustomed to them. We are so used to sin and
conflict, that we don't really understand their depth.
We have developed a system in our own minds that
assigns levels to sin. Some "sins" are worse than others. And of course, my sins are never as bad as the
sins of others. We think that if we've not raped or
murdered someone, then we're not so bad! But that
only reveals how little we understand about the distance we fell in the Garden. We don't understand
how much we have been forgiven by God, and until
we really understand just how much we have been
forgiven by God, we will never have a disposition to
extend that forgiveness to others. When we begin to
understand what God has done for us, when we realize just how great the separation was between us
and God, when we realize that to the holiness and
justice of God our sins were just as obnoxious, broken, fragmented, and desperate as the most horrible
criminal, then we can begin to get our forgiveness of
others into the proper perspective. We like to think
we are somehow better than the Hitlers and Husse-
ins of this world. And yet, sin is sin, separation is

separation, brokenness is brokenness. The blood of Jesus was required just as much for us as it was for the most horrible criminal or psychopath on the face of the earth.

To truly understand why we are called to forgive, we need to learn some important lessons from one of the most powerful parables Jesus taught. Jesus knows that forgiving others is tough. But it isn't impossible, and learning from this parable will make it easier.

LESSON 1: OUR FORGIVENESS WAS VERY COSTLY TO GOD.

Chapter 18 in Matthew's Gospel is all about forgiveness and offenses. Jesus begins the chapter by giving the disciples a picture of the Father's great love.

His goal in this teaching is that the disciples and the readers of this Gospel will discover just how precious each is to the Father. He is hoping they will figure out that the depth of God's love is based, not on perfect performance on the part of human beings, but simple loving childlike trust. There is no need to jockey for position;

Matthew 18:1-5

1 At that time the disciples came to Jesus, saying, "Who then is greatest in the kingdom of heaven?" 2Then Jesus called a little child to Him, set him in the midst of them, 3and said, "Assuredly, I say to you, unless you are converted and become as little children, you will by no means enter the kingdom of heaven. 4Therefore whoever humbles himself as this little child is the greatest in the kingdom of heaven. 5Whoever receives one little child like this in My name receives Me.

there is no need to convince God of our goodness. There is no need to try to connive and control in order to be acceptable to God. He loves us because we are His.

Jesus then, in Matthew 18:6-9, moves to tell the disciples about offense.

Matthew 18:6-9
6 "But whoever causes one of these little ones who believe in Me to sin, it would be better for him if a millstone were hung around his neck, and he were drowned in the depth of the sea. 7Woe to the world because of offenses! For offenses must come, but woe to that man by whom the offense comes! 8If your hand or foot causes you to sin, cut it off and cast it from you. It is better for you to enter into life lame or maimed, rather than having two hands or two feet, to be cast into the everlasting fire. 9And if your eye causes you to sin, pluck it out and cast it from you. It is better for you to enter into life with one eye, rather than having two eyes, to be cast into hell fire."

Jesus wanted them to know that there is a choice when it comes to offending and being offended. Bumping into each other is inevitable. We live in a fallen world and offense is just a part of that fallen condition. I wish I could be more positive, but folks, we just have to accept that fact! We also have to accept the fact that when offense comes we actually do have a choice about how we respond to it. Jesus even gives us the radical and absurd choice that self-mutilation would be a better option than creating more chaos by reacting in vengeance on those that hurt us.

From there, verses 10-14, Jesus tells the parable of the lost sheep.

He is now trying to convince the disciples that God is going to take care of things. He will deal with those that are offensive. He will rescue those that are offended.

A fourth segment, Matthew 18:15-20, deals with preserving unity among believers. He encourages us to deal directly with offenders. He encourages us to let others participate in attempts at reconciliation. He even promises that He will show up when conflict is overcome by forgiveness and unity.

He loves us and we don't have to do anything to gain His love and recognition. He loves us even more than

Matthew 18:10-14

10 Take heed that you do not despise one of these little ones, for I say to you that in heaven their angels always see the face of My Father who is in heaven. 11For the Son of Man has come to save that which was lost. 12 What do you think? If a man has a hundred sheep, and one of them goes astray, does he not leave the ninety-nine and go to the mountains to seek the one that is straying? 13 And if he should find it, assuredly, I say to you, he rejoices more over that sheep than over the ninety-nine that did not go astray. 14 Even so it is not the will of your Father who is in heaven that one of these little ones should perish.

Matthew 18:15-20

15 Moreover, if your brother sins against you, go and tell him his fault between you and him alone. If he hears you, you have gained your brother. 16 But if he will not hear, take with you one or two more, that 'by the mouth of two or three witnesses every word may be established.' 17 And if he refuses to hear them, tell it to the church. But if he refuses even to hear the church, let him be to you like a heathen and a tax collector. 18 Assuredly, I say to you, whatever you bind on earth will be bound in heaven, and whatever you loose on earth will be loosed in heaven. 19 Again I say to you that if two of you agree on earth concerning anything that they ask, it will be done for them by My Father in heaven. 20 For where two or three are gathered together in My name, I am there in the midst of them.

an earthly father loves his children and if someone hurts us, He will see to it that they are dealt with in a judicious fashion. We don't have to take the offense to ourselves; we just need to focus our attention on the Kingdom of God. If one of His little ones strays because of offense, He will drop everything and run after that lost one. And as a reflection of that attitude, He wants us to do the same, to do whatever we can to preserve unity, even by going to an offensive brother or sister in Christ in order to bring reconciliation.[8] The whole first part of Chapter 18 deals with the depth of the Father's love and how to create an atmosphere of love and forgiveness.

Matthew 18:21-22
21 Then Peter came to Him and said, "Lord, how often shall my brother sin against me, and I forgive him? Up to seven times?" 22 Jesus said to him, "I do not say to you, up to seven times, but up to seventy times seven.

All of that then builds to a very convincing climax as Peter responds to the teachings, "Okay Jesus, we get it, we are required to forgive. But tell us this, just how many times are you supposed to forgive?" Then, being in a very gracious and generous mood, Peter adds, "Are we supposed to forgive as much as seven times?" In response to Peter's question, Jesus said, "No, seventy times seven," and then He told the story of a slave who owed his master an unimaginable sum of money. Let's turn our attention first to verses 23-25.

The first thing that would have caught the attention of the disciples and anyone else in that day and age was the amount the slave owed his master. Ten thousand talents was an astronomical sum. The imperial taxes, the taxes

Matthew 18:23-25
23 Therefore the kingdom of heaven is like a certain king who wanted to settle accounts with his servants. 24 And when he had begun to settle accounts, one was brought to him who owed him ten thousand talents. 25 But as he was not able to pay, his master commanded that he be sold, with his wife and children and all that he had, and that payment be made.

levied by the Romans on all of Israel, only totaled 800 talents. By US currency standards of the late 20th and early 21st Centuries, estimates of the worth of ten thousand talents could go as high as $1 billion. So this slave owed his master an unimaginable amount. How a slave could rack up that kind of debt is immaterial. The point is that Jesus gave this number because he wanted the disciples and us to understand that the slave owed the master an amount that simply could not be repaid. No matter how hard he worked, no matter how long he worked, no matter what, he could never repay what he owed. Even if it meant selling himself, his wife and his children, the amount owed simply could not be repaid.

Jesus was trying to teach his disciples (and us) how costly sin is. He was attempting to communicate in unmistakable terms that sin is a debt owed to God. Jesus wanted to make sure that everyone understood the horror of sin. He wanted everyone to know that no matter how small or insignificant we think the sin is, it is still so gross, so horrible, so great a debt, that we can never repay it. Until we see how horrible our sin is, even what we might call little things, we will continue to try to repay God. We will even try to bargain with God, make deals with Him to get our debt reduced. That's what the slave did.

In verse 26 he begs, *"Master, have patience with me, and I will pay you all."* How utterly ridiculous! No one can even figure out how he could have incurred such debt, much less pay it back. And yet, we do much the same when it comes to trying to pay for our sin before God. When we mess up, we go to work trying to make up for sin. We begin to bargain with the Master, "Please, God, I'll do better. I'll start going to church. I'll start paying my tithe. I'll start reading my Bible. I'll even become a missionary. Just let me work off the debt. Let me prove that I can deserve Your forgiveness."

But it doesn't work that way. Sin is so horrible to God that it can't be fixed through human effort. Verse 27 helps us understand the length and width and depth and height of God's love. (cf. Ephesians 3:17-19) The debt was so high that the master said to the servant, "You could never pay back what you owe me, even if you lived to be 1,000. I'll tell you what I'll do, I'll just cancel that debt, and let you go." That forgiveness cost the master one billion dollars.

The forgiveness of sin had a cost, too. It cost God the life of His only Son. I know you've probably seen it before, but it doesn't hurt to see it again and again, because it was an agonizing death. Jesus was led into a public arena and stripped naked. The Roman soldiers mocked, humiliated and fondled the Son of God. Then they blindfolded him and began to slap him around, some hitting him with clinched fists, asking him to prophesy, tell them who had hit him. They pulled his beard out by the handful. They took a crown of sharp Jerusalem thorns and beat it down upon his head. Then they tied his hands, and laced the end of the rope through a brass ring at the top of a post, pulled down and stretched him out until he was standing on tip toe. Then a soldier went to work on him with the Roman scourge. The scourge had many leather thongs; each dipped in sheep's blood and then covered with broken pottery. At the end of each thong was attached a sharp piece of bone or metal. As Jesus was beaten, the scourge tore his flesh. In the end, historians tell us that "these beatings were so severe that bones and organs were left exposed."[9]

Just as he was at the point of death, he was cut down, draped in a purple robe, and made to carry a cross. As he did, people jeered, laughed, and spat upon him. Finally he arrived at the place of the skull. The robe, now stuck to his torn flesh by dried blood, was ripped off, and the bleeding started again. He was thrown down upon the cross piece, and spikes were driven through his wrists. Quickly, efficiently, the cross was hoisted into place, and Jesus' entire weight hung from those two nails. Without delay, his feet were curled under him, one placed on top of the other, and another spike was driven through the instep and out the sole of one foot, into the instep and out the sole of the other, and finally into the wood. And there he hung, suspended between heaven and earth.

His rib cage was expanded in such a way that breathing was difficult and he had to push up with his feet just to get a good breath. Before long, he grew tired; his breathing became shallow, his heartbeat irregular, more like a quiver than a beat. Blood began to pool in his lungs, until there was no room for air. In the end, Jesus literally drowned in his own body fluids.

The sacrifice for our sin was complete, the debt we owed was paid. And there is nothing we can do that will add to what Jesus has already done for us. Folks, if we are ever to learn to forgive, we must learn the first lesson of this parable, that our forgiveness was very costly to God.

LESSON 2: UNFORGIVENESS PRODUCES BONDAGE.

Let's return now to Matthew 18:28-30.

Matthew 18:28-30
28 But that servant went out and found one of his fellow servants who owed him a hundred denarii; and he laid hands on him and took him by the throat, saying, 'Pay me what you owe!' 29 So his fellow servant fell down at his feet and begged him, saying, 'Have patience with me, and I will pay you all.' 30 And he would not, but went and threw him into prison till he should pay the debt.

Can you believe it? The slave just didn't get it. He had been given mercy and forgiveness, but he was unwilling to extend the same mercy and forgiveness to others. The unforgiveness of that small debt put his fellow servant into bondage. I don't necessarily understand it; I just know that when I refuse to forgive, it puts the one I haven't forgiven into bondage. Maybe that sounds like a good thing to you, after all, if someone offends you, that person NEEDS to be put into bondage, right? Not at all, the kind of bondage this text is talking about is a bondage that will prevent you from receiving from the person the kind of response you want. For example, if you are offended and you want the person who hurt you to change, then not forgiving them will put them into a bondage that will keep them from changing. Not forgiving them will put them into the kind of bondage that will cause them to continue in the kind of behavior that caused the hurt in the first place. Remember, the man who owed the money was put into prison where he couldn't earn any money to pay back the debt. So the servant gained nothing by putting the debtor into prison!

Let me explain what I mean by relaying a personal story told by a woman that had been the victim of incest and abuse. I heard the woman tell her story at a conference several years ago. Evan lay in the hospital bed, dying. He was a pitiful sight. None of his family would have anything to do with him. His own children didn't care enough to even check on his condition, much less visit him. In fact, they had not seen him in years. He was consumed with cancer in his mouth and vocal cords, and had been unable to speak for several months.

Twenty-five years earlier, Evan had repeatedly sexually abused his cousin, Linda. After the abuse stopped, Linda held on to hatred and bitterness. She constantly said, "He must pay. I'll not forgive him." When Evan's family finally learned of his actions, they felt the same way as Linda. Then, Linda, along with Evan's family, kept him in bondage for 25 years. And what none of them understood was that as long as they refused to forgive, they were holding Evan in that prison. Bound in the prison of their unforgiveness, he could not change the behavior that had caused him to hurt Linda in the first place.

How would you like to come to the end of your life, face Jesus who had forgiven such horrible personal abuse, and have Him ask, "Why did you keep your brother or sister in bondage? Why didn't you forgive them and set them free?" It's a sobering thought, isn't it? Knowing all Jesus did to pay for our forgiveness, but then refusing to do the same for one who has hurt us or one of our loved ones.

But the offender isn't the only one affected by unforgiveness. It has an even greater impact on us. The conclusion of the parable (Matthew 18:31-34) reveals that the servant that had been forgiven left the master's house and promptly grabbed a fellow servant that owed him money and had him imprisoned. When the master heard what had happened, he arrested the servant he had forgiven and put him in prison and turned him over to the torturers. So, while the servant who owed his fellow slave a pittance was put in prison, the servant who had been forgiven much was put in prison and tortured for his unwillingness to forgive. The lesson to be learned here is that when we refuse to forgive, we begin a process of self-bondage and self-torture that ultimately will destroy us.

Matthew 18:31-34
31So when his fellow servants saw what had been done, they were very grieved, and came and told their master all that had been done. 32Then his master, after he had called him, said to him, 'You wicked servant! I forgave you all that debt because you begged me. 33Should you not also have had compassion on your fellow servant, just as I had pity on you?' 34And his master was angry, and delivered him to the torturers until he should pay all that was due to him.

Evan had problems, but Linda, became a wreck, too. She lived under the care of a psychiatrist for 15 years, and in those 15 years, she made no progress at all. Her life was miserable, empty, and meaningless. In addition to that, her health was failing as she acquired one sickness after another. Because she refused to forgive, Linda was in imprisoned and "delivered to the torturers."

> We can choose to be free, if we will choose to forgive.

But Jesus says none of this has to happen if you will learn the third lesson of this parable.

LESSON 3: FULL FREEDOM COMES WITH FORGIVENESS.

Jesus teaches in verse 35, *"So My heavenly Father also will do to you if each of you, from his heart, does not forgive his brother his trespasses."*

The heart is the center of the will. To "forgive from the heart" is to make the decision to forgive. We can choose to be free and we can choose to set others free, if we will just choose to forgive. Linda, Evan and the family learned that lesson.

One day as Linda prayed, she experienced a vision. She saw herself at the foot of the cross. She saw her cousin, Evan, standing there beside her. Suddenly, the hatred, and anger burned hot within her. Without warning, in her vision she attacked her cousin in a fit of rage. In the midst of the attack, she cried out to Jesus on the cross, "How is it that after all you went through, you can forgive those who have abused you, yet I cannot forgive Evan?"

With that, in the vision, Jesus, beaten, bloody, flesh hanging down in strips, left the cross, and wrapped his loving arms around her. Then Jesus turned to Evan and said, "Look at my face, my back, my hands, my feet, this is what you did to Me when you hurt Linda, but I forgive you."

Then Jesus turned to Linda, showed His wounds to her and said, "I forgave Evan for this, now it's up to you."

Then the miracle occurred, Linda made the choice. She forgave her cousin. In a matter of minutes, the anger, rage and resentment just melted away, and Linda testified, "I felt like a thousand pound weight had been lifted from me."

But it doesn't stop there. Linda began to work with Evan's family, and move them toward forgiveness. The very next day, the family members gathered, and spoke forgiveness to Evan. Instantly, Evan coughed up a phlegm-like substance, and he was able to speak again after three months of silent agony. He only lived a few more days, but he spent the time being reconciled to his family. Forgiveness had set the victim and the offender free from the chains that kept them from becoming all God had created them to be.

RECOGNITION OF PERSONAL SIN

For us to forgive there must be a moment when we recognize just how far we have fallen, but there must also be a time when we realize that God has forgiven us, He has canceled our debt and has restored us to a position of love and respect. Peter is one of the Bible's best examples of this. Peter had lived with Jesus for three years. Many times he had seen Jesus' love restore people that had felt isolated and alone. Many times He had witnessed the power of Jesus' love setting people free from guilt and shame. Many times Peter had watched as Jesus' love renewed hope in people that had lost all hope. And now, Peter would have to use everything he had learned to bring himself back into fellowship, to remove his own guilt and shame, and to breathe new life into dead hope.

On the night Jesus was betrayed, as He was being led off for trial, Peter denied that he knew Jesus. Afterward, Peter avoided Jesus, because he expected Jesus to withhold his love based on Peter's behavior. But once again, just as he had witnessed so many times, Peter came face to face with the lavish love of

Jesus and it dramatically, radically changed him, right down to the very root of his being.

I want you to think about that event, perhaps in a new way. Peter had done something so bad he thought he could never be loved again. Then, he looked into the eyes of the risen Jesus and came face to face with the extravagant love of God. Let your imaginations see this event in a fresh way. Let's take a look at the story as Peter might tell it himself.

Peter Restored: A First Person Musing

My friend John talked much about the lavish love of God. And for me that might be a high and lofty ideal, but it would not have been a reality, if I had not experienced it first hand. All my life I thought that God loved me more when I kept the rules. But all that changed in a moment. We, the other disciples and I, had been with Jesus for three years. Opposition to Him was growing and threats were being made on his life. After celebrating the Passover meal with Him, we left the upper room and made our way to the Garden of Gethsemane for prayer. Suddenly we were surrounded by an angry mob that had come to arrest Him. I was terrified! Things were happening so fast, I couldn't think straight. I tried to defend Him, I pulled my sword and with one blow, I cut off a man's ear. I was poised to strike again, when Jesus grabbed my arm. He looked at me. Oh, the eyes of

Jesus, I didn't know what it was, but His gaze penetrated to my heart.

Ashamed of my actions, afraid of the crowd, I ducked my head and ran. I didn't stop running until I came to the courtyard just outside the house of the high priest. The people gathered there had kindled a fire. I was shivering so I thought I'd warm myself by the fire, but the truth was all the fire in the world could not have warmed me. The cold I felt was from the chill in my soul.

As I sought warmth that would not come, I tried to avoid contact with anyone, but the city was filled with intrigue. Jesus had been arrested, and everyone was guessing his guilt or innocence. Trying to draw me into the conversation, a servant girl asked if I was His disciple. I said I wasn't, and the temperature dropped.

Later, another person, in their speculation about the guilt or innocence of Jesus, asked me if I knew Him. Angrily, I denied it again. And a cold wind seemed to blow. It wasn't many minutes later that Jesus was being moved from the house of the high priest. It was the first glimpse I had gotten of Him since I ran away from Him in the garden. About the time I saw Him, a third person accused me of being with Him. My temper flared, I turned and a third time said, "I do not know Him!" and added a curse.

As soon as the words were out of my mouth, I turned and looked up at the exact same moment He looked at me, and once again the fire in those eyes penetrated to the ice that encased my heart. The pain was excruciating. He had given Himself completely for me; and now, when He needed me most, I denied that I even knew His name. The pain of the moment was so great, that I found myself running from Him again. This time, though, I wasn't running because I was afraid, it was because I was ashamed. Three times I had denied the only person who had ever really loved me. I had deserted Him in the hour of His greatest need. I wept bitter tears until I thought I would be sick.

I wandered the streets of Jerusalem in blind anguish. I was so caught up in my own hell that I forgot all about Jesus. It wasn't until later that afternoon that I was roused from my self-pity, when suddenly, the sky grew dark, the earth began to shake. "Oh my God, what has happened?" I ran toward the hill of Roman execution. And from a distance I saw them, three crosses, and on the middle one . . . the limp, lifeless body of Jesus.

I don't know what happened next. I don't remember sleeping or eating, even going home. The next thing I remember was two days later. Early in the morning, Mary came bursting into the room where John and I were staying. She cried, "They have taken the body of the Lord, and I don't know where they've put it."

Still dazed, John and I ran to the tomb. When we arrived, we discovered that Mary was right, it was empty. I looked around, found the grave clothes, but there was no sign of Jesus' body. All this was too much to take. Suddenly my shame overwhelmed me. I had not told my best friend that I loved him before he died. Not only that, he had heard me say that I didn't even know him. And now, he was dead, the body had obviously been violated, and I would never

> ## I would never be able to tell Him that I really loved Him.

be able to tell Him that I really loved Him. I would never again know His love. I was in utter and hopeless despair.

In the next few days, strange things began to happen. Everyone who had followed Jesus began to report sightings. He was seen everywhere, in the upper room, on the road to Emmaus, in open fields, behind closed doors. I was excited about it, the prospect of Him being alive, but I was still plagued by the horrible guilt of failing Him when he needed me most.

Then one day, almost a month after we found the tomb empty, several of us were fishing. We looked up from our nets and saw a man walking along the shore of the lake. John immediately identified the man as Jesus. Fear gripped my heart. I couldn't let Him see me. Having nowhere to hide, I jumped into the water, putting the boat between Him and me. I didn't know what else to do. I just knew I didn't want Him to see me. The others were excited to see Him, so they rowed toward shore dragging the net bulging with fish behind them. In a matter of seconds they were at the shore. They jumped from the boat and ran toward a charcoal fire where he knelt cooking bread. I heard him yell to the ones in the boat, "Bring some fish!" But they were too excited. They just bailed out and ran to Him. This was my chance. I could make up for denying him. If He wanted fish, I would bring Him fish. Maybe I could show Him I wasn't so bad after all. Maybe He could find it in his heart to love me again.

I climbed back up in the boat and pulled the net in, picked the biggest and best fish I could find and sheepishly carried them toward the fire.

Excited to see Jesus again, everyone was joking and laughing. Everyone, that is, except me. The moment I felt the warmth of that charcoal fire a memory was triggered deep inside. I hung my head, thrust the fish into his hands and immediately withdrew to myself. That's when Jesus came over to me and began to talk.

He asked, "Peter, do you love Me?"

I couldn't look at him. I hung my head in shame, and quietly whispered, "Yes Lord, you know that I love you."

Then he said, "Feed my sheep."

Those words cut like a dagger plunging into my heart. I pulled away from him and walked back to-

---

> Those words cut like a dagger plunging into my heart.

---

ward the fire. Remembering once again that it was beside that same kind of fire that I had hurt him.

He pursued me and asked again, "Simon, do you love me?"

I turned and looked up a little. I didn't dare look into his eyes, even though I could feel them burning right through me, but I did see the scars on his feet and hands. By now, tears were spilling over from my eyes onto my cheeks as I said again, "Yes, Lord, you know that I love you."

And Jesus said, "Then tend my lambs."

"Oh God, how can I?" I thought. "I'm not worthy to do that." And I quickly looked away from his nail scarred hands and feet, back toward that fire. Three times I looked at the fire, and three times I remembered that I had denied him beside a fire. I wanted him to go away, and leave me alone, but a third time He insisted, "Simon, do you love me?"

This time, I spun around, fists clenched, jaws tight, confused that he kept talking about love to me. I was about to tell him to leave me alone, but I made the mistake of looking into his eyes. And when I did, the fire of His love penetrated to my ice-cold heart. He didn't have to say a thing. I saw in those eyes the lavish love of God. All the shame and guilt I had felt for denying Him was gone. Through sobs of joy I said, "Lord, you know all things, you know I love you."

And once again, He entrusted me with the message of His extravagant love when he said, "Feed my sheep."

In that instant, I was new! I looked into the eyes of Jesus and I understood *"what manner of love the Father has bestowed on us"* (1 John 3:1). I finally realized that my relationship with God isn't built on my ability to perform perfectly, it is built on His extravagant love.

The cost of forgiveness is high. It is the price of love. Jesus said, *"Greater love has no one than this, than to lay down one's life for his friends."* (John 15:13)

Then His disciple, John, picked up the same theme when he wrote, *"By this we know love, because He laid down His life for us. And we also ought to lay down our lives for the brethren."* (1 John 3:16)

> My relationship with God isn't built on my ability to perform perfectly, it is built on His extravagant love.

As we realize how much we were forgiven; and as we realize that we were forgiven not because we deserved it, but simply because of the extravagant love of God; then we begin to realize that we can forgive others for the same reason, not because they deserve it, but *"because the love of God has been poured out in our hearts by the Holy Spirit who was given to us."* (Romans 5:5)

Chapter 4

The Choice: Two Doors

Man's purpose is to give God glory. One of the ways that happens is when *"brethren dwell together in unity."* (Psalm 133:1) However, the Devil's goal is to keep us from giving God the glory He deserves and desires. The enemy tricked our first parents into giving that up. He tricked them and continues to trick us into thinking that God is not good, that God is not faithful, and that God is not really even God. He does that in many areas -- finances, health, all kinds of injustices, trials, and troubles. Through the Devil's whisperings, he keeps us off balance spiritually, he clutters our spiritual ears with subtle voices that we have trouble distinguishing from the voice of God, he lures us away from intimacy with God so that we begin to lose our trust in Him. Then, when a crack has formed, the enemy brings irritations and offenses into our lives.

Through fallen heredity, we have an internal bent (a vestige of the Devil's whisperings to Eve) that God doesn't love us as much as He says, that He won't do what He says He will do, and that He can't keep His promises. With that foundation laid, we unconsciously transfer our inner attitudes about God into the area of relational hurt and disappointment.

When irritations and offenses come we think that God can't and won't do anything to bring justice to our particular situation, because He doesn't particularly care about our hurts anyway.

Let me go back to Janet's story for a moment. She was molested by her uncle, the pastor of a church. "A representative of God" hurt her, brought shame on her, and then frightened her into silence. Since I am a product of the 60's, my mind immediately runs to the rock opera, *Tommy*, written and performed by The Who. It's the story of a young man that had all his physical faculties, yet he was deaf, mute, and blind. His problems started when his mother became physically involved with a man other than her husband. Tommy, as a little boy, walked into the bedroom and caught them. These are the lyrics to the song "screamed" at Tommy by his surprised mother and her lover.

> *You didn't hear it. You didn't see it. You won't say nothing to no one never in your life. You never heard it. How absurd it all seems without any proof.*

> *You didn't hear it. You didn't see it. You never heard it, not a word of it. You won't say nothing to no one. No one's gonna know what you know is the truth.*[10]

Those are basically the same words Janet heard from her uncle. When a terribly unjust transgression went undetected and unpunished, Janet began to shut down emotionally, spiritually, and physically. She lost her hearing. She lost confidence in herself. She lost trust in other people. Over the years the enemy convinced her that God was not good if one of His representatives could act like her uncle had acted. He convinced her that God could not be trusted if one of His representatives told her he would lie about what had happened. He convinced her that God certainly didn't love her if one of His representatives could hurt her so. The enemy even convinced her that God was not even God if He couldn't do anything to punish the man that had hurt her.

There must be literally thousands upon thousands of people like Janet. Injustices have come into their lives and the enemy has tempted them away from the truth about God. The enemy has tricked them into changing their understanding of who God is and of how desperately He wants a relationship with the people He created for love. In the absence of a God we can trust, our only option is to hang onto the offense and hope for an opportunity to create our own justice. When we do that bitterness grows, and we end up sick, maybe even sick unto death.

Because of the cross of Christ, we know there is a choice when it comes to dealing with anger and bitterness. We all have anger. In West Texas, the landscape is dotted with feedlots, large pens of cattle being fattened up to send to meat processing plants. Of course, with that kind of operation, there is a terrible stench from the concentration of waste products. Perhaps this is too graphic for some, but it really does illustrate what I'm talking about. The odor in and around a feed lot is horrendous at times, and the communities in closest proximity to these pens are often clouded with stink! I once asked someone that lived in a town surrounded by feedlots how he could stand the smell all the time. He smiled and said, "Oh, you get used to it."

Unfortunately, I fear the same is true of anger. We live in a culture that is so filled with anger that many have become used to it. Wives are angry with their husbands. Parents are angry with their children. Children are angry with their parents and siblings. Parents get angry with umpires and referees at their children's baseball and soccer games. Students are angry with teachers and other students. Employees are angry with their bosses or companies. Citizens are angry with their governments. Races are angry with each other. Countries are angry with other countries. Cultures are angry with other cultures. Religions are angry with other religions. Hey, I even get angry with "that guy" in the car in front of me who sits through two changes of a traffic light! Anger is everywhere! A quick search for the word *anger* on the internet turned up more than 4 million sites that use the word *anger* in some form or fashion. We live on an angry planet that teaches people to either turn their anger inward on themselves or become aggressive toward others. We have just gotten used to dealing with anger in a very human fashion.

Two Doors

In the Bible, the children of Adam and Eve set the standard for the way humans traditionally deal with anger. The story is found in the fourth chapter of Genesis.

God said to Cain, "You have a lot of anger built up. And you have a choice as to what you will do with it. If you make the right choice, you and your sacrifice will be accepted. But if you make the wrong choice, you're in deep trouble."

Genesis 4:1-7

1 Now Adam knew Eve his wife, and she conceived and bore Cain, and said, "I have acquired a man from the Lord." 2 Then she bore again, this time his brother Abel. Now Abel was a keeper of sheep, but Cain was a tiller of the ground.

3 And in the process of time it came to pass that Cain brought an offering of the fruit of the ground to the Lord. 4 Abel also brought of the firstborn of his flock and of their fat. And the Lord respected Abel and his offering, 5 but He did not respect Cain and his offering. And Cain was very angry, and his countenance fell.

6 So the Lord said to Cain, "Why are you angry? And why has your countenance fallen?

7 "If you do well, will you not be accepted? And if you do not do well, sin lies at the door. And its desire is for you, but you should rule over it."

The First Door

The phrase, *sin lies at the door; iand its desire is for you*, is very graphic. The New International Version of the Bible puts it in more colorful language. It says that sin is *"crouching at your door and it desires to have you."* I like that better, because it paints the picture of a huge beast, something like a grizzly bear, sleeping just outside the door of the house. As long as the door is closed and that grizzly isn't awakened, there isn't a problem. But can you imagine what would happen if suddenly the door were flung open and a bucket of scalding hot water were thrown right in the bear's face. I know I wouldn't want to be there! The result would be devastating and destructive.

Unfortunately, that is the choice Cain made. Cain had believed the lies of the enemy. He believed that God was not really good, that God didn't care about his hurt and pain. He believed that God could not be trusted. He believed that God was not really God. And since he already had that mindset, he decided that his only hope for justice was to open the door and fling his scalding hot anger on the sleeping beast of sin. When he did, Abel died.

A key phrase in the above passage is found in verse 3, *"in the process of time."* Something had been brewing in Cain a long time before that fateful day that he met his brother in the field. Like we did with Peter in the last chapter, let's take a little fanciful look at that scene from Cain's point of view. Imagine Cain in his older years, looking back over his life and sharing his heart with us.

CAIN'S CONFESSION: A FIRST PERSON PONDERING

My name is Cain, and I am tired. I have spent my life in regret. The remorse comes from something I did when I was a young man, and it has haunted me day in and day out since that time. I close my eyes to sleep, and there is no peace. I try to distract myself with my work, and it is ever before me. I whistle, and shout, I cover my ears and yet the sound of my brother's blood continues to cry out from the earth. "He being dead still speaks" (Heb. 11:4), and I cannot escape. I live in this restless agony of what I have done -- empty, lonely, and tired.

As I think back on the events leading up to that one act of hateful passion when I turned on my brother and killed him, I am filled with shame. It was something that never should have happened. It was something that could have been prevented -- if I had just listened to my brother. Able constantly told me to trust in God. He constantly told me to stop clinging so much to my possessions and to let God take control of my whole life. He wanted me to have faith.

Have faith!

Ha! Have faith in a God who would place my parents in a magnificent paradise, and then on a whim pull the rug out from under them? Have faith in a God who would promise everything, and then impose restrictions that He knew would be impossible to keep? Have faith in a God who would allow such pain, devastation, and heartache? Have faith in a God who would make my parents work so hard to just barely scrape out a living? Have faith in a God who would cause my mother such discomfort? Have faith in a God who would tell my father to plant a crop only to have it choked out by thorns and weeds? I have seen my father cry all night long as he tried to figure out how he was going to take care of my mother and brother and me. And Abel kept telling me to have faith.

My brother and I were so different. I was the oldest, and the name my parents gave me means, "to acquire", and I lived up to that name. I wanted to acquire, or accumulate everything. I did everything I could to accumulate everything I could, and then cling to all I had gotten, claiming it as my own. I would get and get and get, and would only give very little. I was so selfish. And what I did give was pretty useless anyway.

But my brother was different. His name, Abel, means "breath." I always believed that my parents named him that because he was a breath of fresh air after I was born. But now I have learned that his name reflected his character, just as my name reflected my character.   I was so selfish with the things I called my own, but for Abel everything was as a breath. One minute he had it, and the next it was gone. If I needed anything, or if my parents needed anything, or if God wanted anything, Abel thought nothing of giving away anything he had.

All his possessions were as a breath. He somehow knew that he could only get another after he had let go of the one he had -- and I hated him for that.   I thought he was foolish and irresponsible. He was always saying that God had given him everything, that God had promised to continue to give him everything, and that he didn't need to be afraid to use what God had given him. I thought he was naive to believe that God would supply all his needs. After all, hadn't God promised to take care of our parents' needs only to then kick them out of the garden they had once called home?

The hatred and contempt I had for Abel finally led to his death at my hands. We had been taught from our childhood that every so often -- right after lambing season, and right after harvest -- we were to give the first and the best of our produce to God. And every year, year after year, Abel and I had brought our offering to God. Abel brought the first and best of his lambs because he was a shepherd. I brought my first and best grain because I was a farmer. Abel seemed so content and he gave so willingly and joyfully -- it made me sick.

Every year as I harvested my fields, I hated it more and more. It seemed that every time I talked about God, or heard about God all He ever wanted was more of what I thought was mine. It seemed like such a waste to take my best grain -- grain that would have produced an even more bountiful harvest the next year -- and burn it up on a rock altar for a God who

> It seemed like such a waste to take my best grain and burn it on a rock altar.

didn't care about me, who couldn't be trusted, and who really wasn't even God.

Well, in the process of time, I had taken all I could. Abel was constantly on my back, acting as Mr. Holier-than-thou. God, I felt, was breathing down my neck. My family was struggling to stay alive, and I was trying to figure out what I could cut out that would keep bread on the table for my family and me. That is when it dawned on me. I had seen all that precious cereal go to waste, year after year. And I didn't think I was realizing any benefits from such a waste. So I made a decision.

That year, instead of the usual sacrifice, instead of giving my best to God, instead of giving the first of the new harvest, I decided to keep the new grain. I would use it to plant a new crop, and feed my family. Then, I would give to God the old, stale grain that I had cleaned out of the bottom of the storage bin. It was mildewed, and we couldn't use it anyway. It seemed so logical to me. After all, God had put me in charge of taking care of my family, and He would not want me to neglect that responsibility, either.

With the decision made, I gathered up my offering and headed for the altar of sacrifice. On the way, I ran into my brother Abel. He was carrying a beautiful little lamb over his shoulders. I tried to avoid him, but he saw me, and ran to catch up to me. As we walked together, all Abel could talk about was the great honor it was to be able to give his finest lamb to God. He went on and on, and the more he talked the more nauseous I became. That guy was sickening. Then the wind changed, and he caught a whiff of my mildewed grain and said, "Man, what is that smell? What are you carrying in that clay jar?" I told him it was none of his business. "My offering to God is just between Him and me," I said. I was hoping to avoid a lecture, but I got it anyway.

Abel told me that God deserved only our best. He said that God was so loving and kind and merciful and generous (I hated it when Abel got all sickeningly sweet about God's affections), that he wanted to give back to God in the same way God had given to him. Abel told me that I should give God my best because God had given me His best. He told me that I could trust God. And then he said those words that I hated more than I hated Abel. "Have Faith," he said. And that did it. I decided right then that as soon as we got away from this holy place, and as soon as I

God wanted me to see the bitterness in my heart.

---

could get him alone, I was going to pound him into the ground. I was going to plant him like wheat. Oh, I was enraged!

To add insult to injury, Abel was right. God would not accept my offering. Oh, I know now that it was not because it was mildewed grain, but because God wanted me to see something that was hurting my heart and breaking my relationship with Him. God wanted me to see the bitterness in my heart. God hoped that I would realize that my offering was an exact reflection of my heart. In a very real way, my heart was as mildewed and stinking as the grain I was offering. When God rejected my offering, what was in my heart became very plain. My anger and bitterness boiled over into uncontrollable rage. God must have seen it in my face and he gave me a warning. He said, "Cain, sin is crouching at your doorstep. It desires to have you. But if you really want to, you can master it." I know now that out of His love and kindness and mercy, He was giving me an option. He was offering me a safe way to get rid of my anger.

But I didn't want it. All I wanted to do was get Abel out of my life. I was obsessed with eliminating my goody-goody brother. I caught up to Abel on the way home, and I acted friendly. In fact, hanging my head in artificial remorse, I said, "Abel, you were right. God was not pleased with my sacrifice. And since you seem to know better than I do what God likes, would you come into my field and show me the kind of grain He would want?" I caught him completely by surprise. I hadn't been that nice to him in years. He probably thought that God had finally gotten my attention, that I finally understood God's loving kindness and I was having a change of heart. Abel was genuinely excited about my "conversion." He couldn't wait to get into the field to show me how to please God.

As soon as we got there, he started busying himself around, finding just the right grain; grain worthy of God. He bent down to examine the wheat more closely, and when he did, that gave me a perfect chance to find a big rock. I relive it every day as if it were happening right then. I slipped up behind him, and while he was wrapped up in helping me find the right grain, I raised that rock high in the air, and with all my strength, I brought it down on Abel's head. He never knew what hit him. He fell to the ground, and suddenly I was upon him. Hitting him again and again and again until all the hate I had locked up inside me for all those years came gushing forth in one desperate fit of rage. In less than a minute it was over. Abel, my brother, the man of true faith lay dead in my field.

You know the rest. God found me out and banished me from the very ground He had created to sustain mankind. I had been a farmer, but I no longer would be able to make my living as a farmer. I knew, even before God confronted me, that my actions were wrong, and that I would be punished. But when God took away the only thing I had left, the land, I realized just how wrong I was. I cried out to Him, "My iniquity is more than I can bear, more than could ever be forgiven!"

That is when God showed me mercy, undeserved favor. He gave me a sign that I should build a city where I could take refuge and find some measure of protection. And even though I have been protected, I have not been fulfilled because everything I lost could have been preserved if I had only chosen to obey God instead of allowing the anger inside to have control of me.

Is that really the way it happened? Probably not! But even though I don't know how the scene actually unfolded, I do know that when anger is allowed to brew, *"in the process of time"* it will produce disastrous results.

THE CASUALTIES OF UNCONTROLLED ANGER

Tragically, though, Abel wasn't the only casualty that came from opening the door of self and throwing his anger to the beast. Another casualty was compassion. After the murder,

> *Then the Lord said to Cain, "Where is your brother Abel?"*
>
> *"I don't know," he replied, "Am I my brother's keeper?"*
>
> Genesis 4:9

COMPASSION DIES

Cain had missed the point. He wasn't his brother's keeper; he was his brother's brother. Cain had a responsibility to love Abel, to care for him, to have compassion for him. But because he didn't deal with anger in the right way, he basically said, "I don't care about my brother!" When we choose to open the door and let the beast of sin have our anger, when we harbor bitterness and refuse to forgive, compassion, concern for the well being of others, dies.

"I don't care what happens to someone else, I don't care about their feelings, I don't care why they did whatever it was that offended me all I care about is that my needs are met, and I feel better, even if it's just for a few moments." Compassion dies when we open the door of self-trust and throw our anger on the beast of sin.

PRODUCTIVITY DIES

Genesis 10-12a
"10 And He said, "What have you done? The voice of your brother's blood cries out to Me from the ground.

11 "So now you are cursed from the earth, which has opened its mouth to receive your brother's blood from your hand. 12 When you till the ground, it shall no longer yield its strength to you."

Another casualty that comes from opening the door and throwing our anger on the beast of sin is productivity.

Cain was a farmer. His life was wrapped up in the land. If he had no land, he had no livelihood. No livelihood meant no productivity. When anger arouses the beast of sin, productivity is destroyed and we don't want to do anything good for the person with whom we are angry. Productivity dies when anger awakens the beast of sin.

Friends of mine recently were divorced when the husband became involved with another woman. He left his wife and children and moved in with his new "lover." Of course there was devastation all around. The wife was devastated, and the children were crushed. When the unfaithful ex-husband wanted to visit his children, it took a court order to make that happen. The wife was so angry; she refused to do anything good for the man that had broken her heart and devastated her family, even if it happened to be the legal thing to do. In addition, the wife was so angry that she refused to get a job to support her family. Anger completely destroyed her productivity.

Peace Dies

The third casualty of opening the door and throwing anger onto the sleeping beast of sin is peace.

Cain became a restless wanderer controlled by fear. "... anyone who finds me will kill me." The angry person is always wondering when the next evil will overtake him. The angry person expects the worst of other people. The angry person has trouble trusting others.

Genesis 12b-15.

12 A fugitive and a vagabond you shall be on the earth."

13 And Cain said to the Lord, "My punishment is greater than I can bear! 14 Surely You have driven me out this day from the face of the ground; I shall be hidden from Your face; I shall be a fugitive and a vagabond on the earth, and it will happen that anyone who finds me will kill me." 15 And the Lord said to him, "Therefore, whoever kills Cain, vengeance shall be taken on him sevenfold." And the LORD set a mark on Cain, lest anyone finding him should kill him.

We have seen this on a growing scale since the attack on the World Trade Center in September of 2001. To those who have held on to anger, every person of Middle Eastern descent is suspect. Those holding on to anger tend to think every one of them could be a terrorist just waiting to strike. Innocent people that love America as much as anyone are forced to live in fear because of the anger of some in our nation. Some innocents have even been killed because of people trying to deal with anger on their own. Peace dies when anger awakens sin.

The Second Door

All this happens when we deal with anger after having listened to the voice of the Devil tell us that God doesn't care, God isn't faithful, and God can't do anything about the injustices that have come our way because He isn't really God after all. But God offered Cain a choice, and in doing so He implied there must be another door. When God said to Cain, before he killed his own brother, "If you do well or what is right ...." He was pointing to a choice, a second door, if you will. He didn't have to open the door and throw his white hot anger onto the beast of sin crouching just outside.

Revelation 3:20

20Behold, I stand at the door and knock. If anyone hears My voice and opens the door, I will come in to him and dine with him, and he with Me.

And sure enough in Scripture, there is a second door. The first door is found in the first book, the second door is found in the last book, Revelation 3:20 (see also Revelation 3:8).

When it comes to anger, every person has the choice between these two doors. Outside the door that the Devil would have us open is a sleeping beast of sin. Outside the other door, the door of faith in God, stands Jesus. Opening the door of faith in God makes it possible for Jesus to take your anger. We learned in the last chapter that Jesus paid a very dear price for our sin, He died on the cross so that we would not have to live in the bondage of unrequited anger. It is at this point that we must put the work Jesus did on the cross into effect by opening the door upon which He is knocking.

Colossians 2:13-14

13And you, being dead in your trespasses and the uncircumcision of your flesh, He has made alive together with Him, having forgiven you all trespasses, 14having wiped out the handwriting of requirements that was against us, which was contrary to us. And He has taken it out of the way, having nailed it to the cross.

There are two passages of Scripture that help us here. 1 Peter 5:7 says *"Casting all your cares on Him because He cares for you."* Then Colossians 2:13-14 tells us that when Jesus died, our sin died with Him. We are called to cast all our care, sin, anger, hurt, disappointment, fear, anything that concerns or hurts or worries us, onto Jesus. And the reason we are to do that is because when we do, the negative emotion that threatens to destroy us dies. When Jesus died on the cross, our sin, those we have committed and those we have yet to commit, died with Him. So, pouring anger onto Jesus isn't a denial of anger, it's the only safe and effective way to get rid of it.

We all have anger. Anger is a result of the fall. Anger was handed down to us by our original parents. Cain testifies to that. But when we open the door to faith in Jesus, the anger spills out onto him, and immediately it dies. Then Jesus comes in (as He promised in Revelation), and where anger was, He puts the Holy Spirit. We have fellowship with Him.

Jesus made this the heart of His prayer for us on the night before He was crucified. Jesus prayed for Himself, and then He prayed for His current disciples. Finally, He prayed for all believers from then on, *"21that they all may be one, as You, Father, are in Me, and I in You; that they also may be one in Us, that the world may believe that You sent Me. 22And the glory which You gave Me I have given them, that they may be one just as We are one: 23I in them, and You in Me; that they may be made perfect in one, and that the world may know that You have sent Me, and have loved them as You have loved Me."*(John 17:21-23)

Jesus in us! What a tremendous promise! Suddenly, we become so engrossed with His presence that whatever made us angry seems to lose its power over us.

When our heart fills with anger because of the injustices of life's circumstances, we have a choice. We can listen to the voice of the enemy as he tells us that God doesn't care about us, as he convinces that God will not bring justice to our situation. We can hear that voice, and choose the first door, the door that Cain chose in Genesis, and spill our scalding hot anger onto the beast of sin. And when we do, the

> We become so engrossed with His presence that whatever made us angry seems to lose its power over us.

beast will then awaken and proceed to destroy our compassion, our productivity and our peace. Or we can choose the second door, the door in Revelation behind which Jesus is standing, knocking, begging us to cast our cares on Him, and spill that anger all over Jesus. He will then crucify our anger, and come in and join us in the unjust situations of life. He will replace our anger with the person and power of the Holy Spirit and in the process increase compassion, productivity, and peace.

Chapter 5

The Reality: Getting Personal

I remember living next door to a family in Midland, Texas whose grandfather was a retired military Colonel. It was always interesting whenever he would come for a visit. He kept his car in immaculate condition. It was like a god to him. One day, he and my dad were visiting in the front yard, and I overhead him tell my dad about something that had happened in the parking lot of a hotel while he and his wife were on vacation. It seems that he was sitting in his hotel room, looking out the window. A family pulled in to the parking space next to his car, and when the kids got out, they let the door fly open, dinging his god, his car. Suddenly filled with rage, he let the family get everything into their room, and then when no one was watching, he went outside, took his key and scraped it along the side of that family's car. Can you imagine; a grown man, in his 60s, who did not know how to manage his anger and, therefore, did not know how to forgive?

Most of us would not do what the Colonel did. But what if you had been the one whose car got keyed? Would you be gracious and forgiving? We have seen that our loving heavenly Father has given us the option of "casting all our cares" on Jesus. But what does that look like? What exactly does it mean to cast our cares on Him? In a word, it means to forgive. But forgiveness is tough, and we need some help knowing how to do that. Fortunately, we can find that help from a first century Christian named Philemon. There is a book in the New Testament that bears his name and in it we find a formula for forgiveness.

THREE HEART ATTITUDES

Philemon was a wealthy slave owner from Colossae. Onesimus, a slave who was owned by Philemon, had run away after stealing something of considerable value. As might be expected of someone that wants to become anonymous and hidden, Onesimus ran to the city, probably Rome. He thought he could get lost in the crunch of people. But somehow, under God's unseen hand, Onesimus came into contact with Paul who was imprisoned in Rome. He became a Christian through Paul's ministry, and so he really respected Paul. Paul urged him to return to his master, Philemon, in order to set things right. Onesimus was afraid to do that. The penalty for running away was severe, but the penalty for running away and stealing was death. In an attempt to make returning more acceptable, Paul wrote a letter to Philemon, urging him to forgive Onesimus. In Paul's letter to the Colossian church, Paul lets them know that Onesimus is "a faithful and beloved brother" who is accompanying Tychicus on a mission to discover exactly what is the condition of the church in Colossae. It is from that letter that we gain a clearer picture of what biblical forgiveness looks like.

HEART ATTITUDE #1

Philemon 4-11

4 I thank my God, making mention of you always in my prayers, 5 hearing of your love and faith which you have toward the Lord Jesus and toward all the saints, 6 that the sharing of your faith may become effective by the acknowledgment of every good thing which is in you in Christ Jesus. 7 For we have great joy and consolation in your love, because the hearts of the saints have been refreshed by you, brother.

8 Therefore, though I might be very bold in Christ to command you what is fitting, 9 yet for love's sake I rather appeal to you --being such a one as Paul, the aged, and now also a prisoner of Jesus Christ-- 10 I appeal to you for my son Onesimus, whom I have begotten while in my chains, 11 who once was unprofitable to you, but now is profitable to you and to me.

When Paul says, *"I might be very bold in Christ and command you what is fitting"* (Philemon 8), he is not so much talking about his apostolic authority as he is talking about basic Christian responsibility. He tells us that forgiveness begins as a duty, an obligation, in obedience to God. Paul could have been legalistic. He was God's spokesman, when Paul spoke, people listened. And Paul could have exercised that authority and said, "You want to remain in the church? You want to stay on God's good side? Then do what I tell you, and forgive Onesimus. It is your duty."

In listing that option as one of the possibilities, we discover wherein lies the first level of forgiveness.

Sometimes pure and simple Christian responsibility, duty, obligation to God, is the only way forgiveness can come. We don't feel like forgiving. Everything within us cries out that we shouldn't forgive. Justice demands that something more be done to right the wrong that has offended us or our loved ones. But that is when we have to decide to do the right thing, obey God and forgive.

Most people have heard preacher stories about "Little Jimmy" or "Little Suzy." They are usually fictional stories (perhaps parables) invented to make a point. There is probably some kernel of reality in them, but finding that kernel is impossible. They were told by some preacher at some point in time about a real little girl or little boy, but no one knows for certain who told the story first or what the child's real name is. Anyway, we've all heard those stories and we like them. Better yet, they make the point! So let me share my own "Little Jimmy" story.

Little Jimmy was riding in the front seat of the car while his mother was driving. Jimmy squirmed out of his car seat (now we know that is a recent addition to the story because car seats were probably not even invented when this story originated) and stood in the seat beside her.

Little Jimmy's mother patiently said, "Now Jimmy, sit down. Mommy doesn't want you to get hurt."

Jimmy would sit for a moment, and then he would stand right back up.

"Jimmy, I told you to sit down. Please do as I say!"

He did, but again only for a moment. Traffic was getting heavier and Jimmy's mother was getting more and more nervous and frustrated. Finally, she raised her voice and said, "Now Jimmy, you sit down or I will have to pull over and we'll be late to where we're going."

Little Jimmy didn't budge. He stood there with defiance written all over his face. Mom's eyes met his, she reached over and jerked him down and through clenched teeth said, "Now, son, you sit there and don't you move, or I'll wear you out!"

"Okay," he said, arms folded across his chest, "But I want you to know that I may be sittin' on the outside, but I'm still standin' up on the inside!"

I'm pretty sure that is not a true story. But it clearly illustrates how hard forgiveness can be. We forgive on the outside because of duty, but it takes a while for us to forgive on the inside. And if that is the only way you can do it, then that'll have to do to get us started.

Robert Enright and Gayle Reed, doing research in the area of forgiveness at the University of Wisconsin, Madison, have defined four stages of a process model of forgiveness. They are the Uncovering Phase, the Decision Phase, the Work Phase, and the Outcome / Deepening Phase.[11] It's interesting that during the Uncovering Phase, the offended person "becomes aware of the emotional pain that has resulted from a deep, unjust injury." Then in the Uncovering Phase, the person offended "realizes that to continue to focus on the injury and the injurer may cause more unnecessary suffering... The individual, then, commits to forgiving the injurer who has caused him/her such pain. Complete forgiveness is not yet realized, but the injured individual has decided to explore forgiveness and to take initial steps in the direction of full forgiveness."[12]

HEART ATTITUDE #2

Even though Paul had done no research, he understood that *"what is fitting,"* or duty, is the real starting place of forgiveness. If we are ever to *"cast all our cares on [Jesus],"* we must recognize that it will begin with a decision based on the fact that it is just the right thing to do. At this stage, forgiveness can even have the selfish motive of improving our own well-being. But Paul also knew that wasn't the deepest level out of which forgiveness should occur. In fact, he understood that forgiving out of duty is only the beginning, and so he urged Philemon to move to the second level of forgiveness, trust in God's greater plan.

Perhaps if Philemon could look beyond his anger, his embarrassment, and his economic loss and see God's marvelous plan in Onesimus' running away, then it would be easier to forgive. Onesimus, once a good-for-nothing, thieving slave, lost in his sin, had become a Christian, a believer, a dear brother to Paul and to Philemon. Jesus had turned Onesimus into a real person. And that would not have happened if he had stayed with Philemon.

Philemon 15-16
15 For perhaps he departed for a while for this purpose, that you might receive him forever, 16 no longer as a slave but more than a slave--a beloved brother, especially to me but how much more to you, both in the flesh and in the Lord.

Even in the world of secular research, it has been discovered that trying to find an area of personal growth that resulted from an offense is a helpful device in coming to the point of forgiveness. Dr. Sam Menahem, writes:

> You cannot consciously choose the events of your life, but you can always choose your attitude toward them. A forgiving attitude paves the way for a Spiritual outlook on life. This means that events are looked at as challenges rather than insurmountable obstacles. It means that hidden within even the

direst happenings are the seeds of Spiritual awakening. A serious illness can lead to the blossoming of mature love. An earthquake can lead to selfless devotion to helping injured victims ... Your (so called) enemies were put there to challenge you to develop all the positive Spiritual qualities you can. You are supposed to be working on becoming more loving, forgiving, kind, non-judgmental, faithful etc. If you didn't run into problems you wouldn't be able to develop fully as a Spiritual being.[13]

Several years ago, at a relatively young age, I was diagnosed with Hodgkin Disease, a cancer of the lymph system. When the news came, I was beyond being frightened, I was angry. How could God let this happen? I had a wonderful wife, and three beautiful children. I was at the very beginning of my ministry. I was terribly offended that God would allow this horrible thing to happen to me. And yet now, as I look back at that terrible time in my life and the life of my family, I can see how God walked each of us through that crisis. We all learned so much, and I believe the greatest lesson we learned was that God really loves us. God did not cause me to have cancer; He held me and my family close to His heart and carried us through those frightening times. I've been able to release any offense toward God that presented itself, that is, I've been able to forgive God,[14] because I learned that He will always turn a temporary loss into an eternal gain. It taught me to forgive others, also, by trusting that even though I may never understand it, God always has a greater plan than I can see at the time. Even though I may be hurting, I can forgive because I trust God to bring good to the situation. Of course this can't happen if you have believed any of the lies of the Devil -- that God doesn't love you, that God can't be trusted, and that God isn't really God and can't do what He promises. But if we reject the whisperings of the enemy, then we can trust Him for a bigger plan.

Paul developed that same theme in greater detail in Romans 8:28. *"And we know that all things work together for good to those who love God, to those who are called according to His purpose."* In the Old Testament, the story of Joseph (which we will examine in more detail later) we find a primary example of this principle. Joseph grew up being ridiculed by his brothers. At one time, they threatened to kill him but instead determined to sell him as a slave. While a slave, he was falsely accused of rape and then imprisoned. When he finally did get released, he was elevated to the most powerful position in all of Egypt. Years passed and Joseph's brothers came from Israel to Egypt during a time of drought to buy food. They had to face Joseph who was now in a position to not only put them in jail, but to have them executed! Instead, Joseph looked at his brothers and said,

"Please come near to me." So they came near. Then he said: "I am Joseph your brother, whom you sold into Egypt. But now, do not therefore be grieved or angry with yourselves because you sold me here; for God sent me before you to preserve life. For these two years the famine has been in the land, and there are still five years in which there will be neither plowing nor harvesting. And God sent me before you to preserve a posterity for you in the earth, and to save your lives by a great deliverance." (Genesis 45:4-7)

You see, Joseph trusted that God had a plan beyond what he was able to figure out at the time of the offenses, even though some of the offenses were horrific, and then he was free to forgive.

THE DEMANDS OF FORGIVENESS

Making the decision to forgive is only part of the battle. The decision is akin to making the decision to open a door when someone knocks. Just making the decision does not allow the person knocking to come in. You must actually turn the doorknob and do some work to get the door open. Once we have made the choice to forgive, then the real work begins. There have to be some deliberate actions that follow the conscious decision. The work may include things like striving "to understand the injurer's childhood or put the injurious event in context by understanding the pressures the injurer was under at the time of the offense;" or "a bearing of pain that has been unjustly given. As the individual bears the pain, he/she chooses not to pass it on to others, including the injurer."[15] The injured or offended person may even go so far as to "offer goodwill toward the injurer in the form of merciful restraint, generosity, and moral love."[16]

DEMAND #1

Again, in his letter to Philemon, Paul shows us that true forgiveness involves some work; it has two requirements. First, the debt must be canceled. Whatever it was that Onesimus had stolen[17], Paul offers to pay for it.

> *If then you count me as a partner, receive him as you would me. But if he has wronged you or owes anything, put that on my account. I, Paul, am writing with my own hand. I will repay--not to mention to you that you owe me even your own self besides.* (Philemon 17-19)

He now brings up the fact that Philemon owes his life in Christ to Paul. Paul had been the one that introduced Philemon to Jesus, and his salvation was the result of Paul's evangelistic efforts. Paul was pulling no punches in trying to show Philemon the great debt that had already been forgiven him by Jesus. Philemon had been forgiven far more than Onesimus had stolen. And so Paul is telling Philemon, and us, that true forgiveness demands that we cancel the debt.

THE NEW TESTAMENT CONCEPT

I want to take a little side trail for a few moments to introduce you to a New Testament word. The first active, visible, conscious step in the process of forgiveness is best described by *aphiemi.* According to secular Greek, *aphiemi* can mean: to hurl missiles, to release, to let go; literally, "to open the hand and let go."

There is a story that has been circulating for several years about poachers who engage in the illegal capture and sale of monkeys. Legend has it that they use a very ingenious method of capturing the little creatures without hurting them. And the sad thing is that the method preys on a monkey's own stubborn will. It seems that the hunters will drill a small hole in a gourd and place some food inside. They then attach the gourd to the ground. The hole through which they inserted the food serves a double purpose, it allows the monkey to reach in and grasp some of the food. This is where the monkey's stubbornness works to its demise. Once the monkey has grasped the food, his hand full of food is too large to get out of the hole. But rather than let the food go when the hunters return, the monkey continues to grasp the food and becomes easy prey for the poachers. If they had only "opened the hand" they would have been free; but in hanging on to what they thought rightfully belonged to them, they became enslaved.

I was not convinced of the veracity of this practice, so I wrote to Joe Kemnitz, Ph.D., who is Director of the National Primate Research Center and Professor in the Department of Physiology at the University of Wisconsin, Madison. I asked him about the likelihood of the preceding practice. Here is his response: "I am quite certain that the practice you have described is not commonly used to catch monkeys, but it makes a terrific allegory! Some of us are far too willing to risk something important for a transitory pleasure. Most monkeys that I have known would be sorely tempted by the fruit, but would probably relinquish it if it meant being captured."

How can it be that monkeys are so much more intelligent than humans? They recognize the danger and let go, while we continue to cling to what we think rightfully belongs to us -- bitterness, revenge, anger and hatred, and we become slaves. I have no idea how many marriages have gone into bondage and ruin because one or both partners were unwilling to let go of past hurts and offenses. There is no telling how many children are distant from their parents because parents didn't choose to let go of some wrong a child did. In fact, kids learn at a young age not to tell their parents anything of significance because it will be used against them at some time in the future, maybe even years later! But if there is ever to be real forgiveness, we must choose to cancel the debt, to open the hand of the heart and let go of the hurt.

In addition to letting go, the word, *aphiemi*, was used to call a person to release someone from a contract or some kind of legal relation. In civil government, *aphiemi* requires release from legal punishment, or pardon.[18]

It should be noted that to pardon is "to remove all obligation of payment for a crime." To pardon someone is to say to that person, "You are released from your debt to society for the crime that has been committed."[19] However, it does not make the person innocent, nor does it imply innocence. In fact, a pardon admits guilt! A person who has committed no crime needs no pardon, but only a guilty person can be pardoned. It simply says the person is no longer to be punished, and they can return to society with all its rights and privileges.

On September 8, 1974, President Gerald Ford issued an historic pardon for former President Richard M. Nixon. He had been accused of obstruction of justice in the infamous Watergate Scandal.

There are no historic or legal precedents to which I can turn in this matter, none that precisely fit the circumstances of a private citizen who has resigned the Presidency of the United States. But it is common knowledge that serious allegations and accusations hang like a sword over our former President's head, threatening his health as he tries to reshape his life, a great part of which was spent in the service of this country and by the mandate of its people.

After years of bitter controversy and divisive national debate, I have been advised, and I am compelled to conclude that many months and perhaps more years will have to pass before Richard Nixon could obtain a fair trial by jury in any jurisdiction of the United States under governing decisions of the Supreme Court.

I deeply believe in equal justice for all Americans, whatever their station or former station. The law, whether human or divine, is no respecter of persons; but the law is a respecter of reality.

The facts, as I see them, are that a former President of the United States, instead of enjoying equal treatment with any other citizen accused of violating the law, would be cruelly and excessively penalized either in preserving the presumption of his innocence or in obtaining a speedy determination of his guilt in order to repay a legal debt to society.

He concluded his speech with the following:

I do believe that the buck stops here, that I cannot rely upon public opinion polls to tell me what is right.

I do believe that right makes might and that if I am wrong, 10 angels swearing I was right would make no difference.

I do believe, with all my heart and mind and spirit, that I, not as President but as a humble servant of God, will receive justice without mercy if I fail to show mercy.

Finally, I feel that Richard Nixon and his loved ones have suffered enough and will continue to suffer, no matter what I do, no matter what we, as a great and good nation, can do together to make his goal of peace come true.

Now, therefore, I, Gerald R. Ford, President of the United States, pursuant to the pardon power conferred upon me by Article II, Section 2, of the Constitution, have granted and by these presents do grant a full, free, and absolute pardon unto Richard Nixon for all offenses against the United States which he, Richard Nixon, has committed or may have committed or taken part in during the period from July (January) 20, 1969 through August 9, 1974."[20]

Whether one agrees with what President Ford did or not is immaterial. He did understand that at least part of the nature of forgiveness requires that a debt be canceled. When we forgive, in New Testament terminology, we are not glibly saying that no injustice was performed; we are not saying that the person who offended us is not guilty. We are simply saying that we are no longer going to seek to make them pay for the offenses they have committed against us or our loved ones. When I speak of "paying" I am in no way implying that we have anything at all to do with the legal recourse that could be involved. For example, a child molester or murderer or thief will still be required to serve whatever legal sentence the judicial system hands down. However, we will no longer seek to exact some kind of emotional debt from them, which points to the second part of the first word.

A further concept that follows aphiemi is "to leave behind or leave off."[21] The English phrase: "put it behind you" derives from this concept. Putting an offense behind you, however, means that an offended person must come to a conscious recognition that an offense has been committed. In less sterile language, He must admit he has been hurt and that he is angry! So when Paul says, "*If he has wronged you...,*" (Philemon 1:18) he is moving Philemon to the point of recognition. It is during this phase that "anger and other negative emotions are brought out into the open."[22] Patricia Raybon, associate professor of Journalism at the University of Colorado at Boulder, describes this phase with marvelous clarity and passion.

"...it's one thing to talk glibly about forgiveness. It's another to look hard at what people are trying to forgive. .... Indeed, don't skip too soon ... to the issue of forgiveness. Tarry with [those that have been offended] first on this matter of bone-deep hurt, the real hurt of overt racial pain, for example, and what this injury can mean to people's lives."[23]

It is absolutely imperative that people be allowed, even encouraged, to verbalize their pain as the first visible or conscious step in forgiveness, cancellation of the debt, or "letting go" and "putting it behind you" to use the biblical definition.

John "Buck" O'Neil, a former baseball player for the Kansas City Monarchs of the Negro Leagues, is a shining example of one who has forgiven time after time. However, before he could come to the point of "letting go" or of "canceling the debt," he had to verbalize his pain. In fact, sometimes remaining in an attitude of forgiveness requires a moment of remembering. I'll talk about this more later, but the Old Testament character of Joseph helps us here. The name he gave to his first-born son means "forgetful." Every time he spoke his son's name, he had to remember to forget. In a sense, he remembered his bitterness, he remembered all the injustice done to him by his brothers, and others, and then he remembered that he had made the conscious choice to let it go. That is essential to living in a continued state of forgiveness.

> An attitude of forgiveness requires remembering.

In an interview, Buck O'Neil remembers, "Do you have any idea how many Negro League baseball players were qualified for the Major Leagues? Yet, we couldn't play only because we were black."

He continued his painful memories.

> "Of course, and it wasn't just baseball. There were so many other things we couldn't do... just because we were black. And you have to remember that we weren't the ones who enslaved anyone. They enslaved me in

a certain way, keeping me and my people from so much. Let me say again that, when you think of it, the haters could have been the blacks. Why would you hate me, just because I am an American with black skin? Doesn't the Constitution say that all are created equal? 'All' -- that includes me, too. You know, I went to war for our country. We, not just one race of people, fought Hitler. We fought Hitler for freedom...freedom. When we all came back to this country, what happened? They still treated me like I wasn't supposed to be treated. Yeah, we fought for freedom, didn't we?

We did not fight for this country for the first time during World War II. We fought with you in the Revolutionary War, the Civil War, and World War I. After the fighting stopped each time, what happened? We all fought together for freedom and once we were successful, my people come back and are not given true freedom. Forgiveness becomes essential in the fight for freedom.

I had to deal with forgiveness frequently when in the Navy. I remember an officer who said, "It shouldn't bother you boys to say "sir," because you are accustomed to saying "sir" to a white man.' He was uninformed. What was kind of sad is that he thought it was right to say that. He wasn't trying to be insulting, even though it was. If only he could have put himself in my place. He didn't take the time to know what I've gone through."[24]

It is clear from his comments that there is still pain. The memories are still quite vivid. And yet, he clearly has forgiven those who have hurt him and others of his race. I would contend that without these memories, there would be no real chance at forgiveness.

Dr. Sam Menahem, Ph.D., agrees that recognition is critical to full forgiveness. Often, however, recognition and admission of the emotional pain are not as easy as they might appear. "It is amazing how many troubled people try to minimize the agony they have gone through," he says. "Even in the safety and comfort of a psychologist's office, they try to minimize the pain they have gone through." Then he continues, "It is impossible to truly forgive anyone unless you admit that something went wrong."[25]

Alice Miller, as cited by Dr. Menahem, agrees that recognition is essential to the process of forgiveness. Once the victims have "admitted how bad things were in [their] childhood and allow [themselves] to feel the pain and grieve for the unconditional acceptance [they] didn't get" then and only then will forgiveness be possible. This is equivalent to reliving the offenses. It is important that victims know that being allowed "to feel the pain leads to forgiveness."[26]

It always brings a smile to my face when we moderns have one of those "Eureka" moments and "discover" a new truth that has been stated in the Bible for centuries. Without having modern research psychology to guide him, Paul sought to bring Philemon to the level of consciousness necessary for him to take the first step toward freedom. If he had never admitted the internal pain caused by Onesimus' theft and flight, he would not have been able to reach the goal set by Paul, " *...that you might receive him forever, no longer as a slave but more than a slave--a beloved brother, especially to me but how much more to you, both in the flesh and in the Lord.*" (Philemon 1:15-16)

DEMAND #2

The first demand of forgiveness, canceling the debt, opening the hand and letting go, can be met at the first two levels of forgiveness. A person can let go or cancel the debt either because it is the right thing to do, or because of the recognition of God's greater plan. However, the second demand of true forgiveness will take us to another level altogether. The second demand is to restore the offender. *"If then you count me as a partner, receive him as you would me."* (Philemon 1:17)

Philemon held Paul in highest esteem. Not only was Paul an apostle whom Philemon respected, a believer in Christ, and loyal member of His Body, the Church; but Philemon had been led into relationship with Christ by Paul. Paul was Philemon's spiritual papa! If Paul had showed up at Philemon's house, there would have been great joy. Paul was telling Philemon to treat Onesimus in the same way. Celebrate! Throw a party! Treat him as one you hold in high esteem, see him as family! And that is perhaps the most difficult part of forgiveness, learning to view the offender through new eyes. We have to refuse to make the abuser into something less than human. We refuse to demonize the offender and begin to view that person from a different perspective. In fact, Paul says in 2 Corinthians 5:16, *"From now on, we regard no one according to the flesh."* The Contemporary English Version says it like this, *"We are careful not to judge people by what they seem to be."* And why do we regard no one according to the flesh? Back up once more to 2 Corinthians 5:15 and we find that Jesus *"died for them and rose again."*

Forgiveness can only come when we view even the most horrible

> **2 Corinthians 5:14-17**
> *14For the love of Christ compels us, because we judge thus: that if One died for all, then all died; 15and He died for all, that those who live should live no longer for themselves, but for Him who died for them and rose again. 16Therefore, from now on, we regard no one according to the flesh. Even though we have known Christ according to the flesh, yet now we know Him thus no longer. 17Therefore, if anyone is in Christ, he is a new creation; old things have passed away; behold, all things have become new.*

and cruel and mean-spirited person in the world as someone for whom Jesus died. And so the question we must ask ourselves on a regular basis, especially toward those who hurt or offend us, is, "When I moved into Christ, did I take my eyes with me?" If we are to forgive, we must learn to view people as Jesus does.

> # When I moved into Christ, did I take my eyes with me?

This is not an isolated thought for Paul. Look at just a few verses from his writings.

COLOSSIANS 1:21-22
And you, who once were alienated and enemies in your mind by wicked works, yet now He has reconciled in the body of His flesh through death, to present you holy, and blameless, and above reproach in His sight-

COLOSSIANS 3:9B-10
... since you have put off the old man with his deeds, 10and have put on the new man who is renewed in knowledge according to the image of Him who created him...

GALATIANS 3:26-27
For you are all sons of God through faith in Christ Jesus. For as many of you as were baptized into Christ have put on Christ.

1THESSALONIANS 5:5
You are all sons of light and sons of the day. We are not of the night nor of darkness.

Ephesians 2:1-7
¹And you He made alive, who were dead in trespasses and sins, ²in which you once walked according to the course of this world, according to the prince of the power of the air, the spirit who now works in the sons of disobedience, ³among whom also we all once conducted ourselves in the lusts of our flesh, fulfilling the desires of the flesh and of the mind, and were by nature children of wrath, just as the others. ⁴But God, who is rich in mercy, because of His great love with which He loved us, ⁵even when we were dead in trespasses, made us alive together with Christ (by grace you have been saved), ⁶ and raised us up together, and made us sit together in the heavenly places in Christ Jesus, ⁷ that in the ages to come He might show the exceeding riches of His grace in His kindness toward us in Christ Jesus.

You see, if we are to forgive as we have been forgiven, we must restore the offender, at least in our heart or our perception, to a position of love and respect. Jesus did that for us: once we were darkness, now we are light; once we were dead now we are alive; once we were lost now we are found; once we were not a people now we are a people; we have been restored to a position of love and respect, through no merit of our own! We did nothing to earn it. We did nothing to deserve it! We were elevated "even when we were dead in trespasses."

> We must restore the offender to a position of love and respect. Jesus did that for us

On the night of His betrayal, Jesus washed the feet of the disciples. Then He sat down and taught them, *"For I have given you an example that you should do as I have done to you. Most assuredly, I say to you, a servant is not greater than his master; nor is he who is sent greater than he who sent him."* (John 13:15-16) It seems that we have little choice. If the disciples must become like the Master, and if the Master elevated us to a position we didn't and don't deserve, then we must learn to do the same and see offenders through new eyes!

Interestingly, studies show that a favorable perception of the offender is associated with a greater willingness to forgive; that is, forgiveness is expressed more frequently when the opponent is viewed in a positive light.[27] Dr. Menahem summarizes Robin Casarjian, in her enlightening book, *Forgiveness: A Bold Choice For A Peaceful Heart.*

> " ... many people are just not ready to forgive those who hurt them the most. In this light, she suggests that her readers begin to forgive on neutral ground. That is, she has them first replace their usual judgmental thoughts about strangers with positive loving thoughts. She presents the idea that instead of thinking ill of these strangers, we can remember that they are all part of the greater humanity, and as such are part of God."[28]

Applied to Paul's admonition for Philemon to receive Onesimus as if he were Paul, he is asking Philemon to begin to "see" Onesimus in a new way. That process of learning to think of a person differently helps the healing to accelerate to new and refreshing heights.

I have had the honor of meeting some very special people, many of whom have learned this very difficult lesson of forgiveness. One such person is Peter Loth.

Peter and his wife, Val, work in the healing ministry at the International House of Prayer of Kansas City. The following is an excerpt from his story of forgiveness as told to me in a personal interview.

I grew up in communist Poland after World War II. My "Matka" (Mama) loved me and did all she could to provide food and shelter for the two of us. The city of Torun, where we lived, had been bombed out; most of the buildings were empty shells. Matka and I lived for a while, like so many others, in the underground sewer system. With very little left above ground, we were at least safe and warm. We ate whatever we could find, cats, mice, insects, anything!

My first memory is of men taking me by force away from Matka. I cried and kicked and they answered with their fists. I was taken to an orphanage where 30-40 German children were kept in one room. The Russians and Poles had such hate for the Germans for what they had done during the war that now they vented their anger on these young ones. The orphanages had no beds, one bucket for a potty, and one bucket to hold the food (slop) for all of the children. During the day, we were used as slave labor in the coal mines. At night, we were used for the pleasures of the Russian soldiers and the people that ran the orphanage. Fortunately, Matka's brother was an officer in the Polish army. Many times he rescued me from the orphanage only to see me taken again and returned there weeks later.

There was one girl at the orphanage I will always remember. This girl had a yellow star on her shirt. She would comfort me after I had been abused. She would hold me and tell me, "It's ok; God loves you." One night, the Russian soldiers came to the door and dragged me to the train station. I could hear a noise, like a "pop." As we got there, I could see a pile of bodies, children's bodies. One by one, the Russian soldiers took each of the German children, put a pistol to their head, and shot. I saw my friend, the girl with the yellow star on her shirt, shot in the head and thrown on the pile. When I was to be next, I heard Matka cry out to the Russian officer and I saw her open her dress to him. The officer yelled out a command and I was pushed away, able to go home with Matka. The Russian soldier followed us home to our apartment. Matka had sold her body to save my life.

On my 14th birthday, Matka came to me with tears in her eyes. She held a paper in her hand and told me that she was not my real mother. My real mother was in West

Germany and I would have to leave Poland and go to her. I felt such anger at her, such betrayal! Before I could leave for Berlin, however, I went through months of interrogation and rifle beatings by the Russian KGB. They had received information about my true mother from a U.S. Army base in Germany, and therefore assumed that I, a 14 year old kid, was a spy because I knew someone in the U.S. Army.

Then, after 16 months, I finally met my real Mama. Much to my disappointment, she spoke German and English, I spoke Polish and Russian. I hated her. How could she have left me and gone on to freedom herself? Mama must have seen the hurt and all the questions in my eyes. She unbuttoned her shirt and showed me her back, it was covered with scars. She showed me her breasts, they were mutilated. On her forearm, a number had been tattooed. I understood the pain and abuse she had taken, but I had no understanding of who had done it or why. I wept and embraced my Mama.

Mama had married and African American G.I. in West Germany and had two little girls with him. How I loved my sisters! We transferred to the U.S., to Georgia, in 1959. I was verbally and physically abused from both sides, the whites and the blacks. I was thrown out of the white school and thrown out of the black schools. Once again, I was caught in the crossfire of hatred.

My stepfather became abusive to my sisters. Unable to help them, I would go to my room and cry myself to sleep. One night I could take it no longer; I attacked my stepfather with my fists. He came after me with a chain and beat me severely. I jumped out a window and ran away. Many times during the next 40 years I tried to find my mother and sisters. I even joined the U.S. Army, hoping to find them through military bases. All I found was more discrimination.

Then in 1988, my wife and I were attending a Charismatic Catholic Church in Miami, Florida. We loved what we felt in that church. The church held a powerful weekend of ministry and contemplation for men called the Walk to Emmaus. While I was praying outside in the rose garden, I saw the face of Jesus before me. When I looked into His eyes, He took me on a journey to my childhood. In His eyes, I saw flashes, pictures of my past. All the pain and suffering and despair and fear washed over me like a great flood. Then the Lord told me that He loved me and that He had been with me through all my life. I wept and promised to follow Him and be true to Him all the days of my life.

As I learned to surrender different areas of my life to God, I finally surrendered my mother and my sisters whom I had not seen for so many years. I told the Lord, "You know where they are. Please keep them safe. If You want me to find them, You do it."

Months later, I received a phone call, "Are you Peter? This is your sister, Barbara. Are you a Christian?"

My two sisters were fine, Mama had died that March, the month I had prayed the prayer of surrender. The three of us had a reunion shortly thereafter and they told me that Mama had been in a concentration camp and that she had Jewish blood on her mother's side. I couldn't believe any of it, but after contacting the Red Cross, I was able to confirm that she had been arrested when she was two months pregnant with me. What a shock, I had been born in a concentration camp!

After a while, I began to feel the stirrings of God that I needed to go back to Poland to face it all. When I did, my first stop was Stutthof Concentration Camp. My heart was filled with pain. As we walked to the gas chamber, the ovens, I could feel the pain of the thousands of people who had walked in there so long ago. In the barracks were pictures of the Nazi officers who had worked the camp. Then it came, the audible voice of God calling my name, "Piotrusu! Piotrusu! Piotrusu! You have to do something for Me. Go down on your knees in front of each picture and forgive them."

I argued, "I can't!"

The Voice continued, "You have to forgive them before I can forgive you."

I fell to my knees and forgave each one. I felt so different. I felt as if all of the things I had suffered in my life had been for a purpose, to give God the glory. I had a joy that I had never felt before, freedom in my spirit!

Peter had come to the place that he was able "to invest the faceless criminal with humanity."[29] Kneeling before those pictures of men that had committed such atrocities to him and his family, Peter signaled that he had been able to restore the offenders, the Russians, the Germans, his step father, all his offenders, including his mother who had abandoned him, to a place of love and respect; he saw them through God's eyes.

John "Buck" O'Neil, the former baseball player for the Kansas City Monarchs of the Negro Leagues mentioned earlier, is another grand example of looking at those who offend from a different point of view.

When asked how he could forgive all the tragic offenses committed against him and others of his race, Mr. O'Neil replied, "When you forgive, what you're doing is seeing the person differently. I pray for him, 'God help him. Have mercy on him. He is your child. Yeah. Turn him around.' It's hard to hate a child of God."

Can you imagine the healing that could occur if the victim of injustice and wrong began to have compassion on the unjust? Can you imagine the freedom the victim would experience when they were no longer plagued by thoughts of revenge, bitterness, anger, and fear? It can happen as the offended refuses to demonize the offender and restores him or her to a position of love and respect.

HEART ATTITUDE #3

But that will not happen until we move beyond the "ought to" level and the "God's greater plan" level all the way to level three -- love.

"Therefore, though I might be very bold in Christ to command you what is fitting, yet for love's sake I rather appeal to you." (Philemon 8-9)

Love, divine love, is something that must be imparted as a gift from God. Love is the one identifying trait of those who follow Jesus Christ. He said, *"By this all will know that you are My disciples, if you have love for one another. "*(John 13:35)

Consider the example of Dr. Joon Gon Kim, one of Korea's outstanding educators and Christian leaders. It was springtime and the rain was falling gently as the family was sharing the events of the day. Suddenly, without forewarning or provocation, an angry band of communist guerillas invaded the village, killing everyone in their path. The family of Dr. Kim was not exempt. In their trail of blood, the guerillas left behind the dead bodies of Dr. Kim's wife and his father; he himself was beaten and left for dead. In the cool rain of the night he revived and fled to safety in the mountains with his young daughter. They were the sole survivors.

Dr. Kim is a man of God and he had learned from Scripture to love his enemies and pray for those who persecuted him. But moving from what you know to actually putting it into practice can be tough. Still, the Spirit of God impressed upon him that he was to return to the village, seek out the communist chief who had led the attack, tell him that he loved him, and tell him of God's love in Christ. Talk about a big assignment! In spite of his fear and all that he had to lose, he did what he felt the Spirit had impressed him to do, and God honored his obedience. Dr. Kim's act of love caught the communist leader completely by surprise. But he was so impacted by the love of this man of God, that he knelt in prayer with Dr. Kim and committed his life to Christ. It wasn't long until a number of other communists were converted to Christ and Dr. Kim helped build a church for these and other converts. He later became the pastor of one of the largest churches in South Korea.[30]

When you forgive at the level of love, there are no unsatisfied emotions that will sneak up on you later. Forgiving out of love brings total freedom. People can generally forgive because they ought to; it's the right thing to do. And people will even forgive because they think God might have plans that go beyond their knowledge. But to forgive out of love is extremely difficult because love makes a demand most of us are not prepared to meet. Love demands that we restore the offender to a position of love and respect. And that can be done, as demonstrated by Dr. Kim, Peter Loth, Buck O'Neil, and countless others through the centuries who were willing to allow God's love to consume them and flow through them.

A WORD OF CAUTION

"Whoa! Hold on there, partner!" you might be thinking. "Are you telling me that I have to go back to the husband who abused me and my kids? If that's the case, then I'm not interested." I thought you might react that way. So let me set your mind at ease. A person that has been abused or physically harmed should forgive at a distance, and should not return to a dangerous situation. If a man has beaten a woman, "restoring that man (whether it is her husband or not) to a position of love and respect" does not mean that she should return to her abuser and expose herself again to physical harm. In the biblical context of Philemon, Paul is not asking Philemon to put Onesimus back into his employ. Paul's desire is that Philemon will alter his relationship to Onesimus. He doesn't want them to see their relationship as master/slave any longer, but as brothers in Christ. (Philemon 16)

Forgiveness begins as a mental action in which the offended or hurt party "considers" the offender with the love and respect that is due one who has been created in the image of God, even if the offender doesn't act like he or she was created in that image. That concept is at least a part of what Paul teaches when he demands that the disciple of Jesus Christ *"esteem others better than himself."* (Philippians 2:3) For example, Paul and Barnabas did not always get along so well. At one point in their ministry together, *"the contention became so sharp that they parted from one another."* (Acts 15:39) Paul took Silas with him, and Barnabas went with Mark to do ministry. Then, all four of them were *"commended by the brethren to the grace of God."* (Acts 15:40) They parted from each other in a spirit of forgiveness. They held no grudges. They kept each other in high esteem as brothers in Christ; however, at the moment they could not work together. However, later in his ministry, Paul specifically made this comment, *"Only Luke is with me. Get Mark and bring him with you, for he is useful to me for ministry."* (2 Timothy 4:11) There was a sharp disagreement, but later in life, Paul had restored Mark and Mark had restored Paul to a position of love and respect. They saw each other through the eyes of Jesus.

Yet another example is in the relationship between Peter and Paul. When they were in Antioch, Paul confronted Peter for his hypocrisy. He was requiring gentiles to adhere to Jewish laws in order to be saved. The confrontation took place in a public forum, where Peter would be embarrassed and humiliated. (Galatians 2:11-13) In a very real sense, Paul offended Peter. Although Peter could have held a grudge, later he refers to Paul as *"our beloved brother"* who wrote *"according to the wisdom given to him."* (2 Peter 3:15) These are the words of one who is viewing an offender through the eyes of God. Even though there was no hint of animosity between Peter and Paul, they simply were not called or equipped to work together. Forgiveness calls for us to restore the offender to a position of love and respect in the way we view the offender. Eventually, if we do it right, forgiveness may even make it possible for us to spend time with them and to remain in their presence with great joy.

This biblical principle has powerful implications when applied to the attitude of Christians around the world toward the extremist Muslims who planned and carried out the vicious attacks on the World Trade Center, the Pentagon, the downed airliner in Pennsylvania on September 11, 2001, the bombing of trains and busses in Madrid and London, and dozens of other acts of terrorism. If choosing to view an offender through the eyes of God truly is a biblical

> Love leaves no choice but to make every effort to see even terrorists as created in the image of God.

principle, then it has universal application. If it has universal application, then love leaves no choice but to make every effort to see even those terrorists as created in the image of God. We must view them as persons in need of redemption, too.

A Right View of God

It is obvious that there is not much of the kind of restoration I'm talking about going on. If biblical forgiveness is going to break down, it will probably be at this point. People can let go of an offense be-

cause they know they ought to; they can let go because they trust God to have some kind of larger plan
at work than they are able to see at the time of the offense. But moving into the third level of forgiveness,
forgiving out of love and restoring the offender to a
position of love and respect seems virtually impossible.

The reason it is impossible is because too many
people have the wrong view of God. Most people today see God as mostly mad all the time. They think
He is always sad and grumpy. They believe that He
is just looking for ways to get us to mess up so that
He can punish us. It's as if He has His thumb just
inches away from our heads and the moment we do
something wrong, He's ready to squash us. But when
we look once again at Philemon, we discover that he
had something that is quite rare today. Philemon
worshipped the right God. When Paul commended
Philemon for the *"faith which you have toward the
Lord Jesus"* (verse 5) he included immediately, and
your *"love for all the saints."* He continued, *" we
have great joy and consolation in your love, because
the hearts of the saints have been refreshed by you,
brother."* The only kind of faith that produces that
kind of love, is faith in the God of love, faith in the
God who is always glad, the God who is doing everything He can to keep us in the game or get us back in
the game when we have fallen.

Too many people worship a God that is always looking for a way to count them out, just waiting for them to foul up so He can punish them when they fall. Once again we remember the voice of the serpent in the Garden telling Eve that God wasn't good, trustworthy, or able to really take care of her. The Devil introduced Eve and Adam (and consequently all their offspring) to a grumpy, uncaring, impotent God who will never bring justice to his children. If that is your God, then of course forgiveness won't be easy, or even possible for that matter. But if you have faith in the God who chose you in love, the God who is filled with patience and compassion, the God who is doing everything He can to make it possible for you to enter into the Kingdom, then forgiveness is not only possible, it is exhilarating!

Jonathan, my son, was probably seven years old and I had just bought him a new baseball glove. He loved that thing. He oiled it. He flexed it. He put a ball in the pocket and placed it under his mattress. He loved that new glove and he was treating it well!

I was playing on a church softball team at the time, and the first night we had a game after he got his new glove, he wanted to take it to the ball field and play catch with his friends. I told him I didn't think it would be a good idea. I said, "Jonathan, why don't you leave it home this time? You may lay it down somewhere and some other kid will pick it up." Still he insisted. I said, "What if it gets stolen?" He continued to insist and promised to take good care of it, and so I let him. As we got out of the car at the ball park, I said, "Now be sure to keep up with your glove."

We played the game, then afterward we went across the street to a snow cone stand and everyone got snow cones. Finally, I gathered everyone up and headed home. The ball park was about 20 minutes away from home and so after the snow cones and the travel time, it was at least 45 minutes after the game until we arrived home. Everything was great right up to the moment we pulled into the driveway. Just as the front tire hit the concrete, a little light bulb flashed in Jonathan's head and he blurted out, "Oh no! I left my glove, we have to go back and get it!"

Oh my! You would have thought he had murdered the president. This was the moment I had known was coming and I took full advantage of it. "I told you to keep up with your glove. I knew you would forget it."

"But Dad!" he protested. "Can't we go back?"

"No we are not going back to the ball park, that's 20 minutes away, and besides, someone has probably already picked up that nice new glove and it won't even be there. You get to your room and you think about it. I'm not gonna buy you a glove, the next one you will have to earn the money yourself." I mean I jumped all over him.

I was making a fool of myself, pacing back and forth outside his room, sticking my head in the door every now and then asking, "Are you thinking about it?" Meanwhile, Debbie (my wife) had gotten in the car and headed back to the ball park.

Almost an hour later, Debbie pulled into the drive way. She got out of the car, glove in hand, walked right past me without even looking at me, and quietly pushed open the door to Jonathan's room. She walked over to that little boy who was still sniffling and placed his beloved baseball glove gently on his lap. Then she proceeded to tell him, "You know how you felt when your glove was missing? Well, Jonathan, that's how God feels when you are not close to him. And do you remember how it felt to see that glove and have it back? Well that's how God feels when his children come close to Him."

Did I feel like a heel? Not at all! I felt like something stuck to a heel after a walk through a cow pasture!

Now, which type of God do you have faith in? The "Tom" type or the "Debbie" type? Do you understand what I mean? Too many Christians see God like I was with Jonathan, giving us rules and then just daring us to mess up, almost hoping we will make a mistake so He can crush us or give us some terrible disease. But God is not like that at all. He is more like Debbie was with Jonathan, finding ways to get us back in the game, finding ways to show His compassion, finding ways to include us in His Kingdom, finding ways to fill our hearts with His love. He is constantly looking for ways to give everything we need to restore even the most horrible offender to a position of love and respect. That brings us to a very important question. Does restoring a person, even the 9/11 terrorists, to a position of love and respect undermine justice?

Is Justice Undermined By Forgiveness?

The answer is, "Not at all!" In Romans 12, Paul goes into great detail describing the forgiving behavior that is expected of those who have been given new life in Christ. He tells them to *"bless those who persecute you;"* and continues by telling them not to *"repay anyone evil for evil."* He extends the instruction even further with, *"Do not take revenge, my friends, but leave room for God's wrath;"* and supports his instruction by quoting Deuteronomy 32:35, *"It is mine to avenge; I will repay,"* says the Lord. Paul takes forgiveness to a higher level and reinforces the biblical principle of elevating the offender to a position of love and respect when he quotes Proverbs 25:21, 22: *"If your enemy is hungry, feed him; If he is thirsty, give him a drink; For in so doing you will heap coals of fire on his head."* He then closes his instructions with, *"Do not be overcome by evil, but overcome evil with good."* (Romans 12:9-21)

In the very next section, Paul moves to a teaching about submission to governing authorities. It may appear inappropriate to follow a spiritual lesson on love and forgiveness with submission to secular government. One controversial, curious section reads, *"For rulers are not a terror to good works, but to evil. Do you want to be unafraid of the authority? Do what is good, and you will have praise from the same."* Those instructions are followed by this interesting statement: *"For he* (the governing authority such as a king, emperor, etc.)[31] *is God's minister to you for good. But if you do evil, be afraid; for he does not bear the sword in vain; for he is God's minister, an avenger to execute wrath on him who practices evil."* (Romans 13:1-4)

This explanation implies that Paul's Roman readers may have issued a protest such as, "Wait a minute, Paul! You mean that when we are abused, and misused we are to let the criminal off with no punishment? Is there no room for justice at all? Will no one come to the aid of the oppressed?"

Paul's response assures the people that if they will live in personal forgiveness God will use the governing authorities to exact justice where it is necessary. What a wonderful freedom this brings. The offended party doesn't have the burden of figuring out how much is too much, and how little is too little. There is no need to carry around a grudge. There is no need to always be on alert for the right time to mete out justice. The individual is free to demonstrate Christ-like love and forgiveness with the assurance that somehow, God will avenge any wrongs. The actions of the United States in Afghanistan and Iraq following the events of September 11, 2001, served justice by the governing authorities, thus freeing individual Americans to forgive, to let go of the wrongs and, to see even the terrorists as persons created in the image of God. When a precious child is murdered, it is up to the government to bring justice to the situation, thus freeing the ones who love and miss the child to forgive the murderers!

On an individual basis, for example, when an abusive parent, or a child molester escapes the bar of human justice, we can be assured that God will be the One before whom the offender must stand. God will exact justice from the offender. On first glance, especially from the perspective of the one victimized, that may be exactly what you think you want to see happen. But just a quick overview of Scripture should cause us to pause and remember, *"It is a fearful thing to fall into the hands of the Living God."* (Hebrews 10:31)

In Isaiah we read,

"And they shall go forth and look upon the corpses of the men who have transgressed against Me. For their worm does not die, and their fire is not quenched. They shall be an abhorrence to all flesh." (Isaiah 66:24)

Then we read what happened to Herod in the book of Acts:

So on a set day Herod, arrayed in royal apparel, sat on his throne and gave an oration to them. And the people kept shouting, "The voice of a god and not of a man!" Then immediately an angel of the Lord struck him, because he did not give glory to God. And he was eaten by worms and died. (Acts 12:21-23)

Going further to the book of Revelation we find God pouring out such horrific judgment and darkness that people *"they gnawed their tongues because of the pain."* (Revelation 16:10-11) Those are only a few of the dozens of promises that God will bring justice to all those that appeared to have escaped judgment here on earth.

O hurting and wounded ones, God has not forgotten you. You are so very precious to Him. Look at this:

You shall no longer be termed Forsaken, ..., But you shall be called Hephzibah [My delight]; For the Lord delights in you, ..., And as the bridegroom re-

joices over the bride, so shall your God rejoice over you. (Isaiah 62:4-5)

Since He delights in you, He will hear your case. And the promise to you all is:

He sent Me after glory, to the nations which plunder you; for he who touches you touches the apple of His eye. For surely I will shake My hand against them, and they shall become spoil for their servants. Then you will know that the Lord of hosts has sent Me. (Zechariah 2:8-9)

God will not leave your cry for help unanswered. He loves you and He will fight for you. You are his beloved. You are His precious one. You are the apple of His eye. He fought for you unto death so that you would not have to face an eternity of torment. And that in itself should cause you to ponder, "Do I really want such horror inflicted on any one for all eternity? Do I really want anyone to spend eternity in such a place where 'their worm does not die, and their fire is not quenched'?" No matter what pain they have caused us or our loved ones, we must cry out to God for His mercy to them. We must seek their salvation so they can avoid the depth of justice they may deserve. For in reality, we all deserve the kind of judgment just described and only God's wonderful mercy has rescued us. As followers of Jesus Christ, we cannot withhold from others what we have gained freely from the hand of God.

THE HARDEST PERSON TO FORGIVE

At this point, I hope you are getting to the place where you are glad to forgive those that have offended you. However, there is one person that continues to mess up, one person that continues to disappoint, one person that continues to do offensive things that you just won't forgive. There is one person that you constantly put on probation every time he or she fails. For some reason you can apply these principles of forgiveness to everyone except this one person; and that person is YOU. Somehow, you can cancel the debt of an offense done by someone else; you can even restore someone else to a position of love and respect after they have failed you; you can understand that you are to forgive others in exactly the same way as you have been forgiven by God. But until now, you've not been able to apply those principles to yourself. Now is the time! Think of the worst thing you've ever done; cancel the debt; restore yourself to the position of love and respect; don't spend one minute longer on your self-imposed probation! The cross canceled your debt and restored you to a position of love and respect. Now you do the same and you will be really free!

Chapter 6

The Walk: Staying Free

It was November of 2000. A friend and I were playing around. He was carrying me on his back when he fell forward, causing me to fly over his head. I landed hard on the concrete, creating misalignment in my jaw and back. The pain was unbearable. I had not fully recovered from that injury when, two years later in March, the car I was driving was hit by a drunk driver. I first believed that I was uninjured but the next morning I woke up in excruciating pain. The doctor diagnosed me with severe whiplash. Immediately I began a regimen of physical therapy three to four times a week. I was in constant pain, not only in my back, but all the way through my neck. The new injuries, combined with the yet unhealed injuries from two years earlier caused severe headaches and even breathing difficulties.

During this time my emotions were ones of anger towards God and towards the individuals who had forced my life to be put on hold. Anger turned inward bringing depression and feelings of self-condemnation. I thought, "Surely, I could have done something differently to have prevented the mess I'm in right now!". My depression was turning to hopelessness.

Rebecca Grisham's story is the epitome of resentment. Resentment plainly means to "feel over and over and over and over again." It means "to re-live the event that caused pain or disappointment." Millions of people live every day with the devastating memory of some hurtful or disappointing event. And the re-living of those events is stealing God's joy. It is stealing their ability to give joy to someone else. Resentment, reliving the past hurts, is keeping them from demonstrating the wonder and joy of a relationship with the God whose love burns for them.

God is so taken by us that He describes His desire for us as *"a most vehement flame"* so powerful that "many waters cannot quench it." (Song of Solomon 8:6-7) When He looks upon us, He says, *"You have ravished my heart with one look of your eyes."* (Song of Solomon 4:9) God speaks through Isaiah and reveals that *"the Lord delights in [us]."* (Isaiah 62:4) Jesus even prays that we would know and experience the same kind of love with which God, the Father, loved Him, the Son. There is no doubt that the Father loved the Son. He states it often in the Gospel records. The Father loves the Son! And the Son prays that we will understand and experience the same love that the Father has for the Son! Most of us never realize just how much God loves us, even likes us, because we are too busy re-living past hurts and offenses. But we can experience God's love. We can enjoy life and God's love as we learn one of the most freeing aspects of forgiveness. It's at this point that some would quote the saying, "Forgive and forget." And the truth is we don't forget. We let it go. Eventually, the memory will recede into the background of our consciousness. But we never really forget. If that is so, if we will always remember the offense, then how do we avoid re-living painful events, how do we avoid resentment? We avoid resentment by changing the context of our remembering. Instead of remembering the offense through a cloud of bitterness, we can begin to remember from a place of love and understanding.

Let me explain what I mean by using the life of Joseph from the book of Genesis in the Bible. Joseph teaches us that since we are going to remember the events that have wounded us anyway, we might as well stop seeing them through lenses of pain and bitterness and begin to view them through lenses of love and understanding. Joseph is one of the best examples of how this aspect of forgiveness works because he experienced so much injustice and abuse, and yet he was able to forgive and live in joy.

It is evident from Genesis 37:3-4 that Joseph's brothers hated him because he was the favorite son. They constantly abused him verbally.

Genesis 37:3-4
3 Now Israel loved Joseph more than all his children, because he was the son of his old age. Also he made him a tunic of many colors.
4 But when his brothers saw that their father loved him more than all his brothers, they hated him and could not speak peaceably to him.

Further, his dad used him as a spy against his older brothers. (Genesis 37:12-14)

Genesis 37:12-14
12 Then his brothers went to feed their father's flock in Shechem.
13 And Israel said to Joseph, "Are not your brothers feeding the flock in Shechem? Come, I will send you to them." So he said to him, "Here I am."
14 Then he said to him, "Please go and see if it is well with your brothers and well with the flocks, and bring back word to me." So he sent him out of the Valley of Hebron, and he went to Shechem.

The brothers not only verbally abused him from his childhood; they also threatened to kill him. (Genesis 37:18-20)

Genesis 37:18-20
18 Now when they saw him afar off, even before he came near them, they conspired against him to kill him.
19 Then they said to one another, "Look, this dreamer is coming!
20 "Come therefore, let us now kill him and cast him into some pit; and we shall say, 'Some wild beast has devoured him.' We shall see what will become of his dreams!"

They changed their minds about killing him, and instead they sold him into slavery.(Genesis 37:23-28)

He was transported to Egypt by an Ishmaelite caravan where he was sold to Potiphar, an officer of Pharaoh and captain of the guard, as a household slave. (Genesis 39:1)

While a slave, Potiphar's wife falsely accused him of attempted rape, and had him thrown into prison. (Genesis 39:10-20)

Genesis 37:23, 26-28
26 So Judah said to his brothers, "What profit is there if we kill our brother and conceal his blood?
27 "Come and let us sell him to the Ishmaelites, and let not our hand be upon him, for he is our brother and our flesh." And his brothers listened.

Genesis 39:1
1 Now Joseph had been taken down to Egypt. And Potiphar, an officer of Pharaoh, captain of the guard, an Egyptian, bought him from the Ishmaelites who had taken him down there.

Genesis 39:10-20
10 So it was, as she spoke to Joseph day by day, ... 12 saying, "Lie with me." But he left his garment in her hand, and fled and ran outside. ... 16 So she kept his garment with her until his master came home. 17 Then she spoke to him with words like these, saying, "The Hebrew servant whom you brought to us came in to me to mock me; ... 20 Then Joseph's master took him and put him into the prison, ...

Then, as if that were not enough, a fellow prisoner told him that upon release he would put in a good word for Joseph, which he never did. That left Joseph in prison for two years for a crime he didn't commit. (Genesis 41:1 & 9-14)

Genesis 41:1 & 9-14

1 Then it came to pass, at the end of two full years, that Pharaoh had a dream; and behold, he stood by the river.

9 Then the chief butler spoke to Pharaoh, saying: "I remember my faults this day. 10 "When Pharaoh was angry with his servants, and put me in custody in the house of the captain of the guard, both me and the chief baker, 11 "we each had a dream in one night, he and I. Each of us dreamed according to the interpretation of his own dream. 12 "Now there was a young Hebrew man with us there, a servant of the captain of the guard. And we told him, and he interpreted our dreams for us; to each man he interpreted according to his own dream. 13 And it came to pass, just as he interpreted for us, so it happened. He restored me to my office, and he hanged him."

14 Then Pharaoh sent and called Joseph, and they brought him quickly out of the dungeon; and he shaved, changed his clothing, and came to Pharaoh.

At the age of 30, after interpreting a very strange dream for Pharaoh, Joseph was rewarded and suddenly elevated from the position of prisoner to Prime Minister of Egypt. Finally, after 30 years of living hell, abuse, false accusation, and imprisonment, Joseph's ship had come in. He was in charge, the rains were coming at just the right time, the fields were yielding bumper crops, Joseph met and married a princess, and they had two sons. Everything was right with the world. Joseph was as happy as any man could be. He could finally get on with his life and put the past behind him. If he never saw his brothers again, he would be very happy.

The seven years of prosperity, predicted in Pharaoh's dream and interpreted by Joseph (Genesis 41:25-31) finally came to an end. Famine set in, just as Joseph had predicted. After two years of famine, Joseph's brothers came to Egypt from Israel looking for food. Joseph saw them, recognized them, and every painful memory that had been suppressed for years exploded onto his consciousness with searing pain. And yet, Joseph met his brothers with grace and generosity. He spoke kindly to

Genesis 41:25-31

25 Then Joseph said to Pharaoh, "The dreams of Pharaoh are one; God has shown Pharaoh what He is about to do: 26 "The seven good cows are seven years, and the seven good heads are seven years; the dreams are one. 27 And the seven thin and ugly cows which came up after them are seven years, and the seven empty heads blighted by the east wind are seven years of famine. 28 This is the thing which I have spoken to Pharaoh. God has shown Pharaoh what He is about to do. 29 Indeed seven years of great plenty will come throughout all the land of Egypt; 30 but after them seven years of famine will arise, and all the plenty will be forgotten in the land of Egypt; and the famine will deplete the land. 31 So the plenty will not be known in the land because of the famine following, for it will be very severe."

his brothers saying, *"But now, do not therefore be grieved or angry with yourselves because you sold me here."*(Genesis 45:5)

What? Can you believe that? After all they had done to him, how was he able to respond to them like that? How was he able to keep resentment, re-living those painful events, looking at them over and over again through lenses of bitterness and hatred, from stealing God's dream from him? The answer is found in the names of Joseph's children. From their names, we learn how to change resentment into release. We learn how to stop viewing the offenses of life through lenses of bitterness and hatred and begin to see them through lenses of love and understanding.

Offenses will come. We will remember them. We cannot deny they happened. We cannot bury them. But we can admit that that the offenses were hurtful, even devastating. When Joseph named his first son "Manasseh" that is exactly what he was doing. In Genesis 41:51, we find *"Joseph called the name of the firstborn Manasseh: "For God has made me forget all my toil and all my father's house."*

As I stated in an earlier chapter, the name "Manasseh" means "forget, to vanish from memory." Now that doesn't mean Joseph never remembered the event again. The fact that Joseph named his son "forget" would make that son a constant reminder of what he wanted to forget. So what it really tells us is that Joseph made a conscious choice to see the events in a new light. He didn't deny the past. In verse 51 he admitted that the past had brought him nothing but *"toil"* at the hands of *"his father's house."* But he did make the choice to view it through lenses other than bitterness and hatred. In a sense, he remembered to forget!

This is an example of the "Uncovering Phase" of forgiveness defined by Robert Enright in an earlier chapter. Frederick Luskin, a postdoctoral fellow in the Complementary and Alternative Medical Program at Stanford University makes this observation: "I help people refocus their emotions and think clearly. The way you think about things makes you upset. We hold on to a grudge, thinking that eventually we'll gain control or balance the scales, but it's only hurting us."[32] He encourages his patients to view the negative events in life through new lenses. They do not deny that something negative and hurtful happened; they just view it in ways other than bitterness and anger.

Alice Miller, follows the same line of thinking when she encourages adults that were abused as children "to admit that it really was that bad, and allow yourself to acknowledge the feelings that were too painful and dangerous to feel in childhood." Further, she "believes that forgiveness arises naturally once you have admitted how bad things were in your childhood and allow yourself to feel the pain and grieve for the unconditional acceptance you didn't get."[33] This is exactly what Joseph was doing when he named his first son, "Forget" or Manasseh; he was making a conscious effort to admit the pain of his childhood and then move on.

Let's continue the story of Rebecca Grisham from the first pages of this chapter. More of her story reveals that she had a "Manasseh" experience of her own, on her way to healing. She continues.

In September of 2002, the same year as the car accident, I felt the Lord leading me to move to Kansas City, Missouri to be apart of the International House of Prayer. One week after moving to Kansas City the Healing Rooms that are a ministry of the International House of Prayer began to operate on a regular basis. When I heard about them I decided I had nothing to lose, and that I would check it out. The doctors couldn't do anything for the continual pain and even after much prayer I was still not improving.

A vital part of the Healing Room model is coming to the table of the Lord asking Him to reveal anything in our hearts that would hinder Him from being able to move freely. I was asked to do this as I came the next day for prayer. At first I thought I had nothing in my heart to bring before the Lord but as we continued to pray, the person leading the prayer time asked if I had forgiven the individuals that had caused both of the accidents. That surprised me because I thought I had. But almost immediately, it became evident to me that I had become blind to the anger, bitterness, and unforgiveness, almost as if a wall had been put up around me.

Because confession is a part of the Lord's Supper, I agreed to confess out loud that I forgave them again. As soon as I did the dam behind which I was holding my anger broke. I began to sob as the walls I had built in my heart came crashing down. As the anger flooded out, the presence of the Lord came rushing in to the places my unforgiveness had made off limits to Him. It was then that my eyes were suddenly opened to see what the true condition of my heart had been all along as I held onto anger and bitterness.

As I left the room that day I didn't feel any physical changes. My back and neck and jaw still hurt. However, emotionally I knew the Lord had freed me from the chains of anger and unforgiveness. All the feelings of depression quickly vanished. I was encouraged by the prayer leader to come back again the next day when he felt the Lord would come to me with physical healing. Upon leaving the prayer room, I went to the doctor. He confirmed that nothing had changed, physically. He said my spine was so out of alignment that I couldn't swing my arms in a natural way. He pointed out that one shoulder was considerably higher than the other and that one leg was shorter than the other, all this because my spine was so messed up.

Rebecca had begun to change the way she looked at her injuries and those that had caused them, just like Joseph looked at his injuries differently; he moved on. Joseph's moving on was realized even more as his second child was born and named Ephraim. Ephraim means "fruitful." Free, after having admitted past hurts, Joseph was able to see that God had made him very "fruitful in the land of his suffering." He could now see the blessings that had been there all along. Again, he didn't deny that suffering existed, he readily admitted that things had been hard, but his focus was off the hardships and on the blessings.

So it was with Rebecca. Her story comes to a marvelous conclusion.

> Still in pain, yet with expectancy in my heart, I went back to the healing room the next morning. As soon as the team began to pray while laying their hands on me, I began to feel literal movement in my spine. It felt as though someone had put their hand inside my back and started releasing the tension in the muscles and realigning all the vertebrae. As this shifting was going on in my back I watched and felt my right leg shift

until it was the same length as the left. At the same time, my shoulders began to come into alignment. And as I swung my arms on either side of my body without any problems, I realized that the Lord had indeed come with healing to my body.

The next day, I went back to my doctor, who told me that everything was in perfect order now. That was not surprising, however, because I was no longer in any pain; and I have continued to be free from pain. My neck and back are fine, and I no longer have any headaches or breathing difficulties associated with the accidents. It has been a year since my miraculous healing and I am very aware that the key to my healing was forgiveness.

Finally, she was able to enjoy the wonderful blessings of healing that had been available all along because of the cross of Christ. When you forget, let go, you will begin to experience blessings, fruitfulness.

Now watch this; this is great stuff! In the naming of his sons, Joseph shows us that forgetting past hurts or offenses and seeing the blessings of life are an ongoing, constant process. Every time Joseph mentioned those names he would remember to forget past hurts and to see the present blessings. When he called them to supper, he would remember to forget the past hurts and see the present blessings. When a stranger would ask, "What are the names of your boys?", Joseph would have to remember to forget past hurts and see present blessings.

The point is this, you do not let go of the past just once. You do not see God's blessings just once. Getting rid of resentment, forgiveness, is not something you do once and it's over. Resentment, bitterness, anger will creep in and silently drag you back into bondage if you are not constantly on the alert.

Most of us have had painful events in our past. Couples who desperately want children and are not able to have them find resentment rise up when young unwed teen-aged mothers have more children than they want or can care for. Young mothers who had planned on a career and not children, can feel resentment toward the unexpected child that interrupted their plans. Those who have lost jobs resent the person who fired them or the person who replaced them. Those who have been abused resent the abuser, as much for the purity and innocence that was stolen as for the physical and emotional pain inflicted. Those who have lost loved ones, particularly if the death was long and drawn out, feel resentment toward doctors, nurses, even God. Resentment is rampant in our society. It is estimated that 95 percent of psychological depression is the result of anger that has been ignored or suppressed, that is resentment. And when you consider the booming business of pharmaceutical companies selling anti-depressant medications, it gives you some indication of just how widespread is the problem. A huge portion of our population is consumed with such powerful resentment that it requires medication just to cope. But if you don't want resentment to steal your freedom and joy you must let go of past hurts, focus on present blessings, and do both daily.

Now there is one more little truth that is very helpful here. In the early stages of forgiveness, when the wound is raw and the desire to let go is almost non-existent, making the conscious decision to let go comes first, and all by itself. It is almost impossible to see any good things, to realize any blessings at all as long as bitterness poisons the system. So the more you let go, that is, the more you remember to forget, the clearer you can think and see the blessings of life. But an event happened later in Joseph's life that indicates there is a reversal of order after the initial act of forgiveness.

In the closing chapters of Genesis, Joseph's father, Jacob (who is now called Israel) is nearing death. As was the custom, Joseph brought his sons to Jacob to receive the patriarchal blessing. Joseph placed the boys in front of Jacob so that Manasseh was on Jacob's right and Ephraim on his left. The right hand was symbolic of the primary blessing, and was customarily given to the eldest son. The left hand represented the secondary blessing and was to be given to the younger son. But Israel/Jacob did an odd and unexpected thing. (Genesis 48:12-14)   He crossed his arms and blessed the boys by laying his right hand on Ephraim (blessing) and his left on Manasseh (forget). Even though Ephraim was the younger, he got the   primary   blessing. Remembering blessings will eventually take priority over remembering to forget.

Genesis 48:12-14

12 So Joseph brought them from beside his knees, and he bowed down with his face to the earth. 13 And Joseph took them both, Ephraim with his right hand toward Israel's left hand, and Manasseh with his left hand toward Israel's right hand, and brought them near him. 14 Then Israel stretched out his right hand and laid it on Ephraim's head, who was the younger, and his left hand on Manasseh's head, guiding his hands knowingly, for Manasseh was the firstborn.

Here's the point I want to emphasize. When it comes to ongoing forgiveness, when those little pieces of residual anger sneak back into your consciousness, be sure to give primary importance to remembering everything God has done for you. If you will start by thinking of all the wonderful blessings you have received from the hand of God, then it will be much easier to remember that you have let go of the past hurts, offenses, and injustices that have come your way. In other words, put Ephraim ahead of Manasseh.

A CALL TO INTIMACY

Unless you fall in love with God and cultivate a deep and abiding relationship with Him, forgiveness at the level I have described will be impossible. Jesus hung on the cross and cried, "Father, forgive them," only because He had kept intimacy with His Father. In Luke 13:24-27 Jesus teaches about entering the Kingdom of God. He says,

> *24 Strive to enter through the narrow gate, for many, I say to you, will seek to enter and will not be able. 25 When once the Master of the house has risen up and shut the door, and you begin to stand outside and knock at the door, saying, "Lord, Lord, open for us," and He will answer and say to you, "I do not know you, where you are from," 26 then you will begin to say, "We ate and drank in Your presence, and You taught in our streets.' 27 But He will say, "I tell you I do not know you, where you are from. Depart from Me, all you workers of iniquity.'*

There we see that our place in eternity is determined by intimacy. Peter learned the lesson of intimacy the hard way. Jesus had just fed 5,000 with five loaves of bread and two fish. (Matthew 14:13-21) Following that event, He sent the disciples in a boat to the other side of the Sea of Galilee, while he went into the mountains to pursue intimacy with His Father. After dark, a storm began to blow on the lake and the disciples were working with all their might just to stay afloat. In the midst of that storm, Jesus came to them walking on the water. Like any normal human being, they panicked, thinking they were seeing a ghost. I'm certain I would have reacted as they did, only perhaps even worse! In an attempt to calm them, Jesus said, *"Be of good cheer! It is I; do not be afraid."* (Matthew 14:22-33)

I'm not sure that would have had an immediate calming effect on me, but it seemed to work for the disciples, well, Peter, anyway. So Peter said, *"Lord, if it is You, command me to come to you on the water."* I'm sure he was thinking, "If He can do it, I can do it!" Peter was just that kind of guy. So Jesus told him to come ahead, which Peter did. He walked on the water! But then Peter figured out what he was doing. He felt the wind and felt spray of the waves hitting his face. He looked around at the waves, and immediately sank like a stone, crying out to Jesus, *"Lord save me!"*

Jesus reached out, grabbed Peter, lifted him up, and said, *"O you of little faith, why did you doubt?"* Now some people think that Jesus was scolding Peter, that he had a frown on his face and anger in his voice. But I'm convinced that Jesus was really laughing, literally playing with Peter. I even think Jesus could have faked letting Peter slip back into the water just one time saying, "Oops, hang on there Peter,

I nearly lost you!" And then he let out a big belly laugh. You see, this whole event was not to humiliate these men. They were Jesus' friends. He loved them! He wasn't looking for a way to demonstrate their weakness. He already knew they were weak. What He really wanted to teach them, though, was to keep their eyes on Him.

In the Song of Solomon, the bridegroom (who is really a picture of Jesus, the heavenly Bridegroom) says to his bride (who is representative of the Bride of Christ, the Church); *"You have dove's eyes."* (Song of Solomon 1:15) That is not a reference to their outward appearance; it is, instead, a reference to the way they work. Doves have a type of "tunnel vision." They don't have peripheral vision. They see straight ahead. Neither do they have variable focus. If you've ever watched a pigeon or a dove walk, you notice that their head appears to be thrusting forward with each step. The reason for that is their ability to focus. They stick their neck out, fix their gaze on a object and step toward it, but in order for that object to stay in focus, they have to keep their head in the same position it was in before the step. So it appears that their head is moving backward. Before the next step, the dove will thrust its head forward, refocus, take a step, and keep its head in the same position it was in just before the step. And that action continues with every step a dove takes. In order for a dove to get where it is going, it must keep its eyes fixed on its goal. It can't afford to look to the right or to the left. So when the bridegroom says of the bride, *"You have dove's eyes,"* he was referring to the fact that she has eyes only for him. That is intimacy!

Making the application to Peter and to all disciples everywhere for all time, if we had dove's eyes, if we kept our eyes fixed on Jesus, we would never sink in times of trial. If we kept our eyes fixed on Jesus, we would not notice the offenses that come our way. If we kept our eyes fixed on Jesus, we would not notice when people do irritating things. If we kept our eyes fixed on Jesus, we would have all the grace we would ever need to forgive whatever offenses come our way. In fact, the writer of the book of Hebrews says,

> *1 Therefore we also, since we are surrounded by so great a cloud of witnesses, let us lay aside every weight, and the sin which so easily ensnares us, and let us run with endurance the race that is set before us, 2 looking unto Jesus, the author and finisher of our faith, who for the joy that was set before Him endured the cross, despising the shame, and has sat down at the right hand of the throne of God. 3 For consider Him who endured such hostility from sinners against Himself, lest you become weary and discouraged in your souls.*
> (Hebrews 12:1-3)

How do we "look unto Jesus," or as the NIV puts it, "fix our eyes on" Jesus? We become intimate with Him. We are not distracted by other lovers. Nothing is more important to us than the love of our life, Jesus. We do not love money more than Jesus. We do not love sports more than Jesus. We do not love politics, or entertainment, or travel, or anything this world has to offer more than we love Jesus. And that will only happen as we accept just how much He loves us. As the love of Jesus begins to sink into our understanding, when we begin to experience the width, and length, and depth and height of Jesus' love (Ephesians 3:14-19), we will also realize that His love for us is not based on our performance. He doesn't love us because we do anything. He simply loves us. His love is wide enough to include every race, tribe, nation and tongue. His love is long enough to reach into eternity past and eternity future. His love is deep enough to pursue us even to the very gates of hell. His love is high enough to escort us into the holy presence of God. And wonder of wonders, we get it all completely free! When understanding of the magnitude of God's love begins to penetrate our hearts, oh believe me, we will fix our eyes on Jesus and we will never take them from His beauty. At that time, forgiveness will be no problem at all, for we will be like Him! (1 John 3:2)

1 John 3:2
2 Beloved, now we are children of God; and it has not yet been revealed what we shall be, but we know that when He is revealed, we shall be like Him, for we shall see Him as He is.

Chapter 7

The Urgency: The End of the Age

In the introduction of his book, *Approaching Hoofbeats*, Billy Graham makes the following observation: "I have become more deeply aware of the enormous problems that face our world today, and the dangerous trends which seem to be leading our world to the brink of Armageddon. I also have become more deeply convicted about the responsibility those of us who are Christians have to declare and live the gospel ..."[34]

Ten years later, in 1992, Dr. Graham wrote again, only this time with more urgency. "... there are storms on the horizon. We are plagued by rising debt, growing crime, new expressions of racial and ethnic hatred, disintegrating moral values, sexually transmitted diseases and the AIDS epidemic, the collapse of the traditional family unit, escalating drug and alcohol abuse, and increasingly hostile attacks against the Christian church. Is this all coincidence or is it perhaps a symptom of something else?"[35]

Another 10 years have passed since those words were recorded, and the escalation of evil continues. The twin towers of the World Trade Center in

New York have disappeared in a boiling cauldron of smoke, fire and dust as Muslim terrorists of the al-Quaeda succeeded in delivering a staggering blow to the United States by flying hijacked jetliners into them, as well as the Pentagon, killing thousands. Suicide bombers continue to run unchecked in Israel. Suicide bombers, with ties to Osama bin Laden and the al-Quaida continue to attack sites around the world. Terrorists carried out a successful attack on a passenger train in Spain; hundreds were killed. The United States is at war in Afghanistan and Iraq with the situation continuing to be terribly deadly to all concerned. Growing hostility by Arabs toward the West is the natural repercussion. The Korean peninsula continues to be troubled as North Korea rattles its developing nuclear saber. Bolivia and other parts of South America tremble in social chaos. The Sudan, in Africa, is reeling as the Janjaweed militias are attempting Rwanda-style genocide. French counter terrorism experts are beginning to sound the alarm that the use of chemical weapons is a greater threat than previously suspected. India is on the brink of an AIDS catastrophe. Cities in the U.S. are battle grounds for gangs and drug dealers.

The world is a very dangerous place and it continues to grow more dangerous. I am more convinced every day that we are living in the time Jesus talked about in Matthew 24:4-14.

Many in the Church have the hope that as things are getting worse, Jesus will return and rapture believers out of this world thus preventing undue suffering on behalf of God's people. Some have the view that the Body of Christ will have to endure some of the tribulation period described by Jesus, but half way through the crisis, the Church will be removed to meet Jesus in the clouds. Still others understand the Scriptures to teach that the Church of Jesus Christ will be called upon to give witness to the glory

Matthew 24:4-14

4 And Jesus answered and said to them: "Take heed that no one deceives you. 5 For many will come in My name, saying, 'I am the Christ,' and will deceive many. 6 And you will hear of wars and rumors of wars. See that you are not troubled; for all these things must come to pass, but the end is not yet. 7 For nation will rise against nation, and kingdom against kingdom. And there will be famines, pestilences, and earthquakes in various places. 8 All these are the beginning of sorrows. 9 Then they will deliver you up to tribulation and kill you, and you will be hated by all nations for My name's sake. 10 And then many will be offended, will betray one another, and will hate one another. 11 Then many false prophets will rise up and deceive many. 12 And because lawlessness will abound, the love of many will grow cold. 13 But he who endures to the end shall be saved. 14 And this gospel of the kingdom will be preached in all the world as a witness to all the nations, and then the end will come.

and power of God throughout the tribulation and at the very end believers will be changed to be like Christ in his glorified body. I understand that these are but three of a whole host of "schemes" articulated by biblical scholars. There are many more combinations of thoughts, ideas, and interpretations of the end of the age. I also understand that each of these schemes can be supported by Scripture. Further, I understand that the way I have described these three is quite simplistic, perhaps overly so. But for my purposes, I want to keep it just this simple.

I understand why so many hope that the pre-tribulation rapture people are correct. They are sure they want to be gone when things get really ugly. If the pre-tribulation rapture folks are not right, and the mid-tribulation rapture theory turns out to be correct, that would not be great, but to some it would be better than the third option. Enduring to the end will not be the most pleasant of experiences and does not

---

> If you can make it through the
> terrible times that are coming,
> you will be saved.

---

appeal to the human psyche at all. However, those words of Jesus seem to stand out like ultra-white teeth under a black light. Jesus did say, *"But he who endures to the end shall be saved."* (v. 14)

Just suppose those words mean exactly what they seem to mean, no theological juggling, no hopeful rearranging of the meaning, just plain simple language. "If you can make it through the terrible times that are coming, the great tribulation, you will be saved." Perhaps my approach is a variation on the classic philosophical question, "Is the glass half full or half empty?" I would rather believe that we, the Body of Christ, will have to go through the great tribulation, and then be surprised when a pre-tribulation rapture occurs; than to believe that I will be removed by rapture before things get nasty only to be terrified and horrified when atrocities begin to happen to my family, my friends, and me.

In fact, I believe it is at this point of doctrine that much of the deception and falling away will occur. When solid believers who have served Christ and His Church faithfully for years, believers that have been taught for years that Jesus will rescue His Body from the horror of the tribulation, when those people begin to experience the terror they thought they would escape, questions will arise in their hearts. "Were we lied to?" "Is the Bible true at all?" "Is God really good?" "Is God really faithful?" "Is God really God?" "Was the whole Gospel story just myth and legend?" When solid believers have been staggered by an unexpected blow such as this, then *"many false prophets will rise up and deceive many."* (v. 11)

Aside from the biblical and theological issues that this discussion brings up, forgiveness plays a major role in preventing the deception and ultimate falling away. You will notice from the text of Jesus' teaching that there is a natural progression in the falling away as we come to the end of the age. First, there are a growing number of injustices, (vv. 6-8) wars and rumors of war, kingdom rising up against kingdom, famines, pestilence, and earthquakes. People will begin to ask, "If God is good and faithful why is this happening?" I dare say that question is already being asked with increasing frequency in many places around the globe.

Matthew 24:6-8
6 And you will hear of wars and rumors of wars. See that you are not troubled; for all these things must come to pass, but the end is not yet. 7 For nation will rise against nation, and kingdom against kingdom. And there will be famines, pestilences, and earthquakes in various places. 8 All these are the beginning of sorrows.

Next, Metthew 24:9 indicates that the tribulation will begin to impact us personally. We or our family members will be handed over to suffering. People will really hate us just because we are Christians. It is already happening in much of the world. *The Los Angeles Times* reported that in Basra, Shereen Musa, a Christian woman, was pelted with vegetables to chants of "Shame! Shame!" as she walked with her mother through a market. Shortly after that, Britain's *Daily Telegraph* reported the deaths of Sabah Gazala and Abdul Ahed, both of whom were Christians, who were shot and killed by two Islamic gunmen within ten minutes in separate incidents also in Basra on May 8, 2003. In Egypt,

Matthew 24:9
9 Then they will deliver you up to tribulation and kill you, and you will be hated by all nations for My name's sake.

Naglaa, a Christian convert from Islam, and her husband Malak have been held in prison since mid-February in an effort to force Naglaa to give up her Christian faith. This is definitely the trend; "Christians today are the most persecuted religious group in the world, and persecution has intensified during the past few years. Torture, enslavement, rape, imprisonment, killings ... even crucifixions are among the atrocities perpetrated upon believers around the world, much of them stemming from two ideologies that prevail internationally: communism and militant, politicized Islam."[34] The Dobson group, Focus

> Christians today are the most persecuted religious group in the world.

on the Family, reports that "more Christians have been martyred in this century than in the previous 19 combined." And we have no reason to believe that this trend will reverse. Every indicator points to the escalation of radical injustices aimed at Christians.

That kind of personal injustice will get us really angry. We'll be angry with the people that are perpetrating the injustices. We'll be angry with the governments that encourage it. We'll be angry at the governments that allow it, turning a blind eye toward it in the guise of prudent diplomacy or economics.

We'll be angry at the God who allows it to continue. In fact, extreme offense is the third step in the progression toward falling away. (Matthew 24:10) These natural disasters and personal attacks, all of them unjust, will have the potential to create in us offense so powerful that we will do whatever we deem necessary to restore justice to the situation. Many will take the law into their own hands. Many will even succumb to the fourth step in falling away as a very human attempt to restore justice, betrayal. (Matthew 24:10) Christians will turn on each other. We will begin to turn in other Christians to the authorities under the promise that those same authorities will make it easier on us if we will just cooperate with them. The action of betrayal will of course escalate into the sixth step toward falling away, hatred will grow from believer to believer (Matthew 24:10). Into the context of offense, betrayal, and hatred will step a series of false prophets that will easily deceive (Matthew 24:11) believers and lead them into open rebellion against God and utter contempt for the Body of Christ. (Matthew 24:12)

> **Matthew 24:10-12**
> 10 And then many will be offended, will betray one another, 10 And then many will be offended, will betray one another, and will hate one another. 11 Then many false prophets will rise up and deceive many. 12 And because lawlessness will abound, the love of many will grow cold.

Perhaps I paint a picture that you would rather not view. But I think the Bible is very clear and we must prepare to face the great tribulation. If we are to stay strong and resist deception by false prophets, we need to stop the process at the first place possible. So where is that? It is quite clear that we are not able to do anything about the international injustices that will occur. We can't stop wars. (I do not discount the power of prayer. I am part of an intercessory prayer ministry that has seen untold numbers of divine interventions in world affairs. But I speak of human effort alone.) Diplomacy and human wisdom will go only so far and will never be able to eradicate war, Jesus promises that. We have no control over kingdoms fighting each other. Neither do we have any control over natural injustices like famine, pestilence, and earthquakes. We don't have any way to stop being arrested and persecuted for our faith in Christ (except to renounce Him which is not an option). It appears that the first, maybe even the only place that the falling away can be stopped is at the point of offense.

It is imperative that the Body of Christ learn to deal with offense by forgiveness now. If we are unable to let go of the injustices that come our way in this age, how will we ever be able to stand when things get really bad? For those of you that have endured terrible treatment, rape, abuse, molestation, murder of a loved one, racism, etc., I do not seek to minimize the trauma and devastation you have received at the hands of others. But as we come closer to the end of the age, we need to seriously evaluate where we stand in the arena of forgiveness. Are we prepared to forgive, no matter what?

Not long ago, I sat with a dear brother that had just received news of unbearable sorrow. His 12-year-old daughter had called and told him that her mom, his ex-wife, was taking her and her brother to Germany for three years. Since the wife had sole custody of the children, there was not a thing he could do to stop her. What made it even worse was the fact that they were leaving the next morning. He didn't know for certain where they were at the time of the call; a hotel room in some undisclosed city is all he knew. He could not see them, he could not hug them, and he could not do anything but tell them over the phone that he loved them. The conversation ended when the mom, his ex-wife, took the phone from the child and hung it up without a word.

Standing beside him, my hand on his back, I felt my friend's shoulders heave with sobs, his face buried in his hands, and a circle of friends comforted him and cried out to God for wisdom, revelation, intervention, justice, clarity of thought, peace, and most of all, forgiveness. We all prayed that he would be able to forgive his ex-wife for doing such a mean-spirited thing.

That event triggered a whirlwind of thoughts, not the least of which related to the day a demon-possessed dictator, the anti-Christ, will rule the world. He will commit atrocities beyond our wildest nightmares. One of the things that will happen will be government sanctioned kidnappings. In order to better control the population, this anti-Christ will capture the children of dissidents and threaten torture, mutilation, and death if we in the Body of Christ don't submit to his authority. There will, of course, be other methods used, but this will be one of the most effective. When that happens, will we be able to stand like Christ and forgive? Will we be able to

> One of the greatest demands of the end of the age is a spirit of forgiveness.

look into the heavens like Stephen, see the throne of God and forgive those that perpetrate injustice upon us? One of the greatest demands of the end of the age is a spirit of forgiveness.

Oh Body of Christ, learn now to deal with offense. Learn now to forgive so that when the day of tribulation comes you will be able to stand. The prophetic promise of Jesus is true, *"But he who endures to the end will be saved. And this gospel of the kingdom will be preached in all the world as a witness to all the nations, and then the end will come."* (Matthew 24:13-14)

When we learn to forgive, when we love in the midst of hatred, when we forgive in the midst of injustice, the world will then know that the love with which God the Father loved Jesus the Son is also in those of us who call Jesus Lord. And then, praise God, we will all behold the glory that Jesus had before the foundation of the world! (John 17:24-26)

John 17:24-26

24"Father, I desire that they also whom You gave Me may be with Me where I am, that they may behold My glory which You have given Me; for You loved Me before the foundation of the world. 25O righteous Father! The world has not known You, but I have known You; and these have known that You sent Me. 26And I have declared to them Your name, and will declare it, that the love with which You loved Me may be in them, and I in them."

End Notes

1 Hindu Passages (available from http://website.lineone. net/~andrewhdknock/Hindu.htm)

2 Islam On Line; "Forgiveness: Islamic Perspective" (available from http://www.islamonline.com/cgi-bin/news_service/spot_full_story.asp?service_id=696)

3 Albuquerque Zen Center; "Practicing Forgiveness in the Land of Judgment" (available from http://azc.org/dharma-talk.php4?id=9)

4 Confucius; (available from http://www.superquotations. com/qq.asp?criteria=Forgiveness)

5 Eliezer Abrahamson, Forgiveness: A Halachick Perspective (available from http://members.aol.com/lazera/forgive. htm)

6 Mortir, Forgiveness and Wicca, part 2: How To Forgive (available from http://members.aol.com/Ecclasia1/forgiveness2.html)

7 Alfred Edersheim; The Life and Times of Jesus the Messiah, (Macdonald Publishing Company, McLean, Virginia; 1883, 1886) Appendix XVII, 784. The Mishnah continues to explain that, in order to involve guilt, the thing carried from one locality to another must be sufficient to be entrusted for safekeeping. The quantity is regulated: as regards the food of animals, to the capacity of their mouth; as regards man, a dried fig is the standard. As regards fluids, the measure is as much wine as is used for one cup, that is, the measure of the cup being a quarter of a log, and wine being mixed with water in the pro-

portion of three parts water to one of wine - one-sixteenth of a log. As regards milk, a mouthful; of honey, sufficient to lay on a wound; of oil, sufficient to anoint the smallest member; of water, sufficient to wet eyesalve; and of all other fluids, a quarter of a log. It has been calculated by Herzfeld that a log = 0.36 of a litre; 'six hen's eggs.' As regarded other substances, the standard as to what constituted a burden was whether the thing could be turned to any practical use, however trifling. Thus, two horse's hairs might be made into a birdtrap; a scrap of clean paper into a custom-house notice; a small piece of paper written upon might be converted into a wrapper for a small flagon. In all these cases, therefore, transport would involve sin. Similarly, ink sufficient to write two letters, wax enough to fill up a small hole, even a pebble with which you might aim at a little bird, or a small piece of broken earthenware with which you might stir the coals, would be 'burdens!' Passing to another aspect of the subject, the Mishanah lays it down that, in order to constitute sin, a thing must have been carried from one locality into another entirely and immediately, and that it must have been done in the way in which things are ordinarily carried. If an object which one person could carry is carried by two, they are not guilty.

8 There is a dramatic difference in forgiveness and reconciliation. I have purposely kept the discussion so far specifically on forgiveness. Reconciliation involves both the offender and the offended. Forgiveness involves only the heart attitude of the one who has been offended. In some cases, reconciliation is impossible; for example, the offense may be of such a nature that the offender is incarcerated and face to face reconciliation is impossible. Or a parent may have abused a child and then that parent died before reconciliation was possible. In either case, the offended person needs to develop a heart for forgiveness.

9 <u>International Standard Bible Encyclopedia</u>, (Grand Rapids: Wm. B. Eerdmans, 1988) 4:359.

10 Pete Townshend, Rock Opera: Tommy, 1969 (lyrics available at http://people.netscape.com/pinkerton/who/Tommy/tommy.tab.html#DidntHearIt)

11 Robert Enright and Gayle Reed, Process Model (Department of Educational Psychology, University of Wisconsin, Madison); available at http://www.forgivenessinstitute.org/html/process_model.htm; Copyright © 2003 International Forgiveness Institute, Inc.

12 ibid.

13 Sam Menahem, Ph.D. (<u>All Your Prayers are Answered</u>. Chapter 7, "How To Forgive Your Enemies"); available at http://www.drmenahem.com/prayers_chapter.htm (07-11-2004)

14 The concept of forgiving God may raise some questions. The concern comes from the fact that God is perfect and could never do anything that requires forgiveness. And while that is true, the nature of offense is such that a person doesn't really have to do anything wrong or offensive. All that has to happen for offense to occur, and thus forgiveness to be needed, is for a person to perceive that another has committed an injustice against them. Saying that I forgave God does not imply that God did anything wrong, it only means that in my emotionally vulnerable state, in my sinful brokenness, I simply perceived that God did something wrong, or better stated, He neglected to do something right (prevent me from getting cancer). In that case, I needed to forgive God, even though He had done nothing wrong.

15 Rick Tripp, "Exploring Faith Today" (available at http://www.christianity.co.nz/forgive5.htm; March 28, 2002)

16 ibid. Enright and Reed

17 There is absolutely nothing to indicate what was stolen. It could have been valuable jewelry, it could have been Philemon's dignity. No one knows

18 <u>Theological Dictionary of the New Testament</u> (TDNT); ed. Gerhard Kittel. Wm B. Eerdman's, Grand Rapids, 1976. 509-512

19 ibid.

20 President Gerald R. Ford's Remarks on Signing a Proclamation Granting Pardon to Richard NixonSeptember 8, 1974. (available at http://www.ford.utexas.edu/library/speeches/740060.htm 07-11-2004)

21 ibid. TDNT

22 Robert Enright; "Proposed Activities Within the International Forgiveness Institute," p. 6. (avaialbel at http://www.dpo.uab.edu/~pedersen/a20.htm) (07-11-2004)

23 Patricia Raybon; "Beyond Bigotry: Adding Action to Forgiveness," (available at http://www.forgiveness-institute.org/ifi/periodical/wof_sample_article3.html) (07-11-2004)

24 An Interview with Buck O'Neil; (available at http://www.forgiveness-institute.org/ifi/periodical/wof_sample_article2.html, 2001) (07-11-2004)

25 Sam Menahem; "All Your Prayers Are Answered," Chapter 7, p. 1 (available at http://www.drmenahem.com/)

26 ibid.

27 Murray Bradfield; Journal of Management, Sept, 1999; "The Effects of Blame Attributions and Offender Likableness on Forgiveness and Revenge in the Workplace." (availlable at http://www.findarticles.com. July 23, 2001)

28 Menahem, p. 2

29 A Campaign for Forgiveness Research, forgive.org, October, 1999

30 Rick Tripp, "Exploring Faith Today."

31 Parenthetical comment mine

32 Joan Passarelli, <u>Los Alto Town Crier</u>, April 21, 1999; (available at http://www.losaltosonline.com/latc/arch/1999/16/YHealth/2research/2research.html)

33 Menahem, ibid., 4.

34 Billy Graham, Approaching Hoofbeats (Waco, Texas: Word Books, 1983), 11.

35 Billy Graham, Storm Warning (Waco, Texas: Word Books), 7-8.

36 Perry L. Glanzer, Focus on the Family (3/1/98 recording)